ASYLUM WITHOUT WALLS

ASYLUM WITHOUT WALLS

DR. IVAN GULAS

SALISBURY & YORK
ACADEMIC PRESS
London - New York - Melbourne

Published by MirageQuest, Inc., dba
Salisbury & York Academic Press
London · New York · Melbourne

Printed in the United States of America

Paperback ISBN: 978-8-218-89110-7

This book is a work of nonfiction. The clinical examples presented are fictionalized composites created to illustrate key concepts clearly and support understanding in an educational context. Any resemblance to actual persons, living or deceased, is purely coincidental.

All images are original, licensed, or AI-generated illustrative representations created solely for educational and editorial purposes.

For information about bulk orders, permissions, or academic use, please contact:

Salisbury & York Academic Press

Info@AsylumWithoutWalls.com

AsylumWithoutWalls.com

10 9 8 7 6 5 4 3 2 1

First edition, January 2026

DEDICATION

For Beth, for a lifetime of love and partnership.

For our children, Kimberly and Jordan, who grew into remarkably kind and generous people, for Kip, who has enriched our family beyond measure, and for Kimberly P., for becoming an important part of our family.

And for Sophie, Alex, and Norman, you are our greatest joy and our brightest hope for the future.

TABLE OF CONTENTS

INTRODUCTION

This book reflects over fifty years of clinical observation, research, and reflection on America's treatment of the severely mentally ill.

I wish to acknowledge the use of artificial intelligence tools in the preparation of this manuscript. AI assisted with organizing research materials, refining prose for clarity, and generating the illustrative images that appear throughout the book. These tools proved valuable in the mechanical aspects of producing a work of this scope. However, the clinical insights, historical interpretations, policy critiques, and reform proposals are entirely my own the product of decades of practice, study, and witness to a crisis that continues to unfold on American streets.

No algorithm taught me what I learned in those locked wards in Ohio, or what I see today driving through Los Angeles. No technology can replace the knowledge that comes from sitting with a patient whose mind has betrayed them, or from watching a family torn apart by an illness our society refuses to treat. That knowledge, and the moral urgency it demands, is what I have tried to convey in these pages.

PROLOGUE
A CLINICIAN'S WITNESS

I write from a particular vantage point. I am not a deinstitutionalization activist who fought to empty the hospitals, nor a homeless advocate who works among the encampments. I am not a policy researcher compiling statistics from a distance. What I offer is something different: the perspective of someone who evaluated patients in a state psychiatric hospital in 1971 and who now, over fifty years later, drives through Los Angeles seeing remarkably similar symptoms unfolding on our streets.

My professional background shapes how I see this crisis. I earned my doctorate in Clinical Psychology from Ohio University and I am Board Certified in Clinical Psychology by the American Board of Professional Psychology. I completed my clinical internship at Beth Israel Hospital, Harvard Medical School. For years, I provided clinical services at a private inpatient psychiatric hospital in Boston and in my private practice. Later, I expanded my training to include neuropsychology, and together with a psychiatrist colleague, I founded Boston Neuropsychology Services. Our evaluation and consultation practice included inpatients at McLean Psychiatric Hospital, one of the nation's premier psychiatric institutions. I also served on the faculty at Harvard Medical School for over two decades.

I understand how the brain works and how it fails. When I see a woman on Spring Street talking to invisible tormentors, I don't see a "homeless person." I see specific patterns of neural dysfunction that I've evaluated countless times. The difference is that my patients had beds, medication, and someone monitoring their condition. The woman on Spring Street has a sidewalk.

This book, The Asylum Without Walls, draws on both personal witness and historical research. The chapters on ancient civilizations, medieval Europe, and the Kirkbride era synthesize scholarship from historians and medical researchers' work, I have tried to present them accurately while acknowledging I am not a historian. The chapters on deinstitutionalization, the legal transformations, and the current crisis draw heavily on what I personally witnessed: the locked wards I walked, the patients I evaluated, the discharge process I observed as it unfolded, and the transformation of Los Angeles that I've watched over more than twenty-five years of living here.

I have also examined how other nations approach this population the Netherlands, Germany, Italy, Japan, and others.

What I found was not that these countries solved severe mental illness, but that they share a principle America has uniquely rejected: that someone must always be responsible for ensuring the severely mentally ill do not deteriorate unprotected in public. This international perspective informs the proposals I offer. The solutions are not theoretical; they exist and function in other developed democracies.

I write extensively about advances in brain imaging and what neuroscience now reveals about severe mental illness. This reflects my background in neuropsychological assessment the clinical discipline that bridges brain function and behavior. Modern imaging confirms what clinicians have long observed: that psychosis, anosognosia, and impaired judgment have biological substrates we can now visualize. This matters because it transforms the moral argument. We are no longer speculating about whether someone "really" can't recognize their illness; we can see the compromised brain regions that make insight impossible. Yet our legal frameworks have not incorporated this knowledge. Courts continue to treat refusal of treatment as an informed choice, even when we can demonstrate that the brain structures required for informed choice have been damaged by the illness itself.

The statistics and cost estimates I cite throughout this book are approximations based on published reports, government documents, and professional literature. I am a clinical psychologist, not a statistician or academic researcher. I have made every effort to be accurate, but these figures should be understood as directional indicators, illustrations of broader patterns, and the scale of what has happened rather than independently verified data points suitable for scholarly citation. Where I cite numbers, my purpose is to convey trajectory, not to provide authoritative figures. This is not a research paper or formal policy document. It is a witness account informed by clinical training, a perspective I hope adds something that pure research cannot: the observations, insights, and recommendations of someone who was there at the beginning and has watched the consequences unfold across five decades.

In 1971, as a psychology intern, I spent months evaluating patients in an Ohio state hospital, witnessing the realities of institutional life, the complexity of severe mental illness, and above all, the human beings caught within that system. The same symptoms, the same struggles, the same profound disconnection from reality that I observed then I see now on the streets of Los Angeles, but without walls, without beds, without even the flawed refuge those institutions once provided.

A woman experiencing severe psychiatric distress while living unsheltered.

My career took an unexpected turn from clinical practice to technology and entertainment, but I never stopped seeing the world through clinical eyes. Every drive through Venice, Hollywood, or downtown Los Angeles is a diagnostic exercise I cannot turn off. The psychiatric symptoms are unmistakable to anyone trained to recognize them. What's changed is not the illness it's our response to it.

I am now seventy-nine years old. I will not see this crisis resolved in my lifetime. But I can bear witness to what I have seen across five decades, name what I have seen, and describe what I believe must be built to replace the asylum without walls that we have created. My hope is that the insights and recommendations I propose here, new legal standards that replace the failed "imminent danger" test, therapeutic communities that restore dignity while providing protection, and a system built around the principle that responsibility cannot be escaped, do not end up gathering dust on a shelf.

I also hope this book reaches readers who are in a position to advocate for change and who have the courage to champion what we know must be done, against all the forces that perpetuate the comfortable fictions we prefer to hear rather than the difficult truths we need to confront.

The people dying on our streets cannot wait for us to become comfortable with the solutions that might save them.

What I have come to understand across these five decades is that America's failure is not one of resources or knowledge. Other developed nations with fewer resources and facing the same clinical realities have built systems that work. The difference is not capacity but structure. In the Netherlands, in Germany, in Japan, someone is always responsible for ensuring the severely mentally ill receive care. Responsibility cannot be escaped.

America's system is uniquely structured so that responsibility is always escapable. Families cannot compel treatment. Hospitals discharge patients to nowhere. Courts defer to "autonomy" even when the brain structures required for autonomous decision-making have been destroyed by illness. Police transport people to emergency rooms that release them within hours. Everyone can point to someone else; no one is accountable when a human being dies on the sidewalk. This book is an attempt to name that failure and to describe what a system built on inescapable responsibility might look like.

How did this happen?

How did we go from institutions that, however flawed at least provided shelter, medication, and monitoring, to a system that leaves severely mentally ill human beings to die on sidewalks in the richest nation on earth? How did we convince ourselves that this abandonment represents progress, that watching someone rot in their own waste constitutes respecting their autonomy?

These are the questions this book will answer.

The journey begins long before Athens State Hospital, long before the community mental health movement, long before the legal revolution that redefined abandonment as liberty. It begins with humanity's oldest question about the broken mind: What do we do with those who cannot care for themselves?

We will trace how different civilizations answered that question from the bimaristans of the Islamic golden age, where musicians played for psychiatric patients in garden courtyards, to the witch trials that burned mentally ill women as servants of Satan. We will examine America's own attempt to answer it: the Kirkbride asylums that represented genuine therapeutic ambition before they collapsed into the snake pits that rightly horrified reformers.

We will follow the arc of deinstitutionalization, the emptying of state hospitals that was supposed to liberate patients into community care but instead scattered them to streets, jails, and early graves. We will examine the legal revolution that made intervention nearly impossible, the financial incentives that made discharge irresistible, and the cultural forces that made any form of institutional care politically radioactive.

We will look beyond our borders to nations that faced the same challenge and built systems that actually work. the Netherlands, Germany, Italy, and Japan, asking what they understood that we refused to learn.

And we will confront what fills our streets today: the suffering, the violence, the families in quiet agony, the medieval diseases returning to American cities. We will examine what neuroscience now reveals about severe mental illness, knowledge that transforms the moral calculus of intervention, and why our legal framework has refused to incorporate what our imaging technology has proven.

Finally, we will describe what must be built: the infrastructure, the legal standards, and the systems of care that could replace the asylum without walls that we have created.

Before I can do that, I must take you back not to 1971, but much further. The severely mentally ill have always been with us. They have always required an answer. Understanding the answers humanity has tried before the compassion and the cruelty, the insight and the willful blindness is essential to understanding where we are now and what we must do differently.

That history is where we begin.

CHAPTER 1
MADNESS THROUGH THE AGES

The woman arguing with invisible tormentors on a Los Angeles street corner would have been treated very differently in other times and places. A thousand years ago in Baghdad, physicians would have taken her to the bimaristan, the hospital, where musicians played soothing melodies while doctors prescribed treatments based on careful observation. Five hundred years ago in Europe, they would have burned her as a witch. In ancient Greece, she might have found sanctuary in a temple of Asclepius, where physicians would have treated her mental affliction as a disease, not possession.

Today, in the richest nation on earth, we walk past her.

The severely mentally ill have always existed. In every civilization, every era, every culture, there have been people whose minds fractured beyond their ability to care for themselves, people who heard voices no one else could hear, saw visions no one else could see, believed things manifestly untrue with unshakeable conviction. This is the inconvenient truth that shapes everything in this book: some portion of humanity, roughly 1–2% across all cultures and all times, lacks the cognitive capacity to live safely without structured care.

Mental illness is not a social construct, not a failure of will, not a product of capitalism or family dysfunction. It is a medical reality as old as humanity itself.

What changes isn't the existence of severe mental illness. What changes is how societies respond to this unchanging reality. Every civilization has had to answer the same uncomfortable question: What do we do with those whose logic, problem-solving, and grasp of reality have failed them? Do we see them as cursed, diseased, or dangerous? Do we confine them, care for them, or abandon them? Do we consider them our responsibility or someone else's problem?

The answers reveal what societies truly value and what they're willing to ignore. America's current approach of spending billions while watching the mentally ill die on its streets is historically unusual. It's neither inevitable nor universal. It's a choice, made deliberately, to deny an ancient truth., To understand how we arrived here, we need to step back and see the long arc of humanity's struggle with madness.

What follows is that history. Not a comprehensive survey that would require volumes, but rather a selective journey through the moments when humanity got closest to understanding severe mental illness, and the long periods when it willfully forgot those lessons. It's a story of cycles:

compassion followed by cruelty, medical insight followed by superstitious regression, societies building systems of care only to abandon them a generation later.

If there's a pattern in this history, it's this: humanity repeatedly discovers that the severely mentally ill need structured, humane care in specialized facilities. Societies build those facilities. They work, imperfectly but genuinely. Then they undermine them through underfunding, overcrowding, and neglect. Eventually, they abandon them entirely, scattering the mentally ill back to the streets and jails. Then, a generation or two later, shocked by the visible suffering, societies rediscover the same truth and begin building again.

We're in one of those abandonment phases now. Understanding how we got here requires understanding how often we've been here before.

MESOPOTAMIA AND EGYPT: WHEN THE GODS WERE TO BLAME (5000–1550 BCE)

Long before anyone spoke of synapses or neurotransmitters, ancient civilizations were already struggling with minds that had disconnected from reality. Five thousand years ago, a Mesopotamian physician pressed his stylus into soft clay, creating one of humanity's first medical texts. Among recipes for treating wounds and fevers, he described a condition he called bennu a patient who talks to himself, laughs without cause, refuses food, and walks the streets naked. The symptoms are unmistakable: what we would now call acute psychosis.

His prescribed treatment reveals the ancient world's understanding: supernatural explanation combined with practical intervention. "Fumigate him with qannu-plant. Perform the incantation 'Evil demon, get thee hence.' Make an amulet of carnelian and lapis lazuli." Madness was attributed to gods, spirits, or demons, but it was still something to be treated, not ignored. Mesopotamian tablets also make clear that families bore responsibility for their insane relatives. If a man "was seized by the god" their phrase for madness, his family was expected to confine him at home, protect him from harm, and seek treatment from physician-priests who specialized in mental afflictions.

This established a pattern that would repeat through history: family care as society's default solution. It worked adequately when families had resources, failed catastrophically when they didn't, and always placed enormous burdens on relatives who never asked for them.

Ancient Egypt followed similar patterns. Their medical papyri describe conditions that sound remarkably like depression, mania, and psychosis. The Ebers Papyrus, dated to 1550 BCE, prescribes treatments for someone whose "heart is sick": botanical medicines, dietary changes, and religious rituals. For Egyptians, the "heart" was the seat of thought and emotion, so a sick heart encompassed what we would consider psychiatric as well as physical distress.

What's notable about both cultures is this: despite attributing mental illness to supernatural causes, they didn't simply abandon the afflicted. Families bore primary responsibility, but temples and healers provided support. The mentally ill weren't left to wander the desert. There were problems to be managed, even if the management was often ineffective.

These early Mesopotamian and Egyptian approaches predate the biblical world of Israel and the philosophical medicine of Greece. They remind us that long before anyone spoke of ethics or neurons, societies still had to decide: Do we contain these people, care for them, or cast them out?

ANCIENT ISRAEL: THE SEED OF AN ETHICAL FRAMEWORK

Against this backdrop of temple rituals and family confinement, ancient Israel added something new: a durable ethical framework for how a community should regard those whose minds had failed them. Jewish civilization was ancient. Abraham walked around 1800 BCE, Moses led the Exodus around 1300 BCE, King David ruled around 1000 BCE, placing the biblical tradition after the earliest Mesopotamian and Egyptian medical texts, but before the mature Greek and Roman medical systems. Its distinctive contribution was not an early medical theory of madness, but an ethical architecture that proved remarkably resilient.

The most detailed discussions of mental illness in Jewish tradition emerged over centuries from biblical texts through the Talmud (compiled in the 3rd–6th centuries CE) to medieval physicians like Maimonides in the 12th century. What follows spans this entire arc, showing how one tradition maintained ethical clarity about mental illness across thousands of years while surrounding civilizations cycled between insight and brutality.

Biblical texts mention King Saul's episodes of what we might call severe depression or psychosis. The First Book of Samuel describes "an evil spirit from the Lord" troubling him supernatural language, certainly, but the response was remarkably practical: music therapy. Young David played the harp, and "Saul would be relieved and feel better." Elsewhere, figures like Nebuchadnezzar are described in states that read like prolonged psychosis or delirium living outside, losing basic self-care, reality splintered.

More importantly, the Torah established foundational principles: mentally ill individuals, while exempt from certain religious obligations they could not fulfill, retained their place in the community and their fundamental human dignity. There is no suggestion that they cease to be full persons. Families bore primary responsibility for care, but the community had obligations too. This principle that the vulnerable were a collective responsibility, not disposable burdens, would influence medical and ethical thinking across cultures for millennia.

The Talmud contains extensive debates about mental illness, particularly regarding legal capacity and community responsibility. The rabbis weren't physicians but legal scholars trying to answer practical questions every society must confront: When is someone too mentally ill to be held responsible for their actions? Who must care for them? What are their rights? Can they recover?

Jewish law defined a shoteh as someone whose mental illness rendered them legally incompetent. The Talmud describes observable behaviors indicating severe mental disturbance, wandering in dangerous situations, showing no fear of death, and destroying one's own property without awareness. The focus is relentlessly functional: is this person able to understand, to choose, to act responsibly?

Here is what's remarkable: even those deemed legally incompetent retained fundamental human dignity and rights. They couldn't be held legally responsible for their actions, but they remained members of the community entitled to care and protection. Legal incapacity did not erase personhood.

Crucially, the designation wasn't permanent or all-or-nothing. A person could be considered shoteh regarding some decisions but competent for others. Someone might lack the capacity to manage property but retain the capacity to participate in religious rituals. The framework recognized that mental illness existed on a spectrum and could fluctuate over time, insights that modern psychiatry would take centuries to rediscover.

Jewish law also placed clear obligations on the community to care for the mentally ill. The principle of tzedakah, often translated as charity but literally meaning justice or righteousness, meant that caring for vulnerable community members was a matter of legal obligation, not optional kindness. If a family couldn't provide care, the community's charity funds were required to step in. No one was to be abandoned to wander or starve.

The most influential Jewish physician was Moses Maimonides (1138–1204 CE). Born in Spain, forced to flee anti-Jewish persecution, eventually settling in Egypt, where he served as court physician to the Sultan, Maimonides was one of the greatest minds of the medieval world. He wrote extensively on medicine while also being one of Judaism's greatest legal and philosophical authorities.

In his medical writings, Maimonides emphasized the connection between physical and mental health. He prescribed music, pleasant environments, and engaging conversation for patients with melancholy. He recommended exercise, a proper diet, and avoiding excessive worry. For severe mental disturbance, he acknowledged that confinement might be necessary but only to prevent immediate harm, and always with the goal of eventual restoration to the community.

His legal writings addressed mental illness with remarkable sophistication. He distinguished between temporary mental disturbance and chronic conditions. He discussed how illness might affect different mental faculties differently. Someone might lose reasoning ability but retain emotional capacity. He emphasized that mentally ill individuals retained their essential humanity and dignity regardless of their symptoms.

Perhaps Jewish tradition's most important contribution wasn't specific treatments but ethical principles that remained consistent across millennia: mental illness was medical, not moral; the afflicted retained personhood and dignity; community bore responsibility for care; capacity could fluctuate, and recovery was possible; treatment should aim for the highest level of function each person could achieve. These weren't just beautiful ideals; they were legal obligations embedded in the halakhic system that governed Jewish communal life.

The irony is profound: Jewish communities, often persecuted and confined to ghettos, maintained ethical and legal frameworks insisting that even the most disturbed individuals deserved dignity, care, and eventual reintegration. Meanwhile, as we'll see, the Christian majority outside the ghetto walls would later burn mentally ill women as witches.

ANCIENT GREECE AND ROME: THE BIRTH OF MEDICAL UNDERSTANDING (400 BCE–200 CE)

Then came the Greeks, and everything changed.

Around 400 BCE, Hippocrates, the father of Western medicine, proposed a revolutionary idea: mental illness had nothing to do with demons or divine punishment. It was a disease of the brain, no different in kind from a broken leg or infected wound. "Men ought to know," he wrote, "that from the brain, and from the brain only, arise our pleasures, joys, laughter, and jests, as well as our sorrows, pains, griefs, and tears. . . . It is the same organ which makes us mad or delirious, inspires us with dread and fear . . . brings sleeplessness, inopportune mistakes, aimless anxieties, absent-mindedness, and acts that are contrary to habit."
This was radical. Not possession. Not punishment. Disease.

Hippocrates developed the theory of the four humors: blood, phlegm, yellow bile, and black bile. Health required these humors to be in balance; illness resulted from imbalance. The theory was wrong in its specifics, but right in its fundamental insight: mental illness had physical causes and required medical treatment.

Greek physicians prescribed treatments based on this understanding. For melancholia: exercise, a moderate diet, music therapy, and what they called "psychological treatments" we'd call it talk therapy. For mania: cold baths, quiet environments, dietary restrictions. For severe cases requiring confinement, they recommended humane conditions rather than chains and beatings.

Greek society built temples dedicated to Asclepius, the god of healing, where the mentally ill could receive care in tranquil, therapeutic settings. These weren't prisons or warehouses. They were sanctuaries, places of refuge where families could bring relatives who'd lost their minds, knowing they'd be treated with dignity.

Roman physicians continued and expanded this tradition. Celsus, writing in the 1st century CE, recommended occupational therapy for mental illness, keeping patients engaged in activities suited to their condition. Soranus of Ephesus, writing in the 2nd century CE, provided remarkably modern-sounding advice: mentally ill patients should be housed in pleasant rooms, given meaningful activities, and allowed visits from family. Restraints should be used only when absolutely necessary and never as punishment.

This Greco-Roman period represents a high point of ancient understanding. Mental illness was a disease. The mentally ill deserved medical treatment and humane care.

Society had obligations to those who couldn't care for themselves. These insights, achieved through observation, reason, and empiricism, wouldn't be rediscovered in Europe for more than a thousand years.

MEDIEVAL EUROPE: THE RETURN OF DEMONS (500–1500 CE)

With the fall of Rome and the rise of Christianity, Europe's understanding of mental illness regressed catastrophically. The medical model vanished. Demons returned.

The early Christian church taught that the body was a vessel for the soul, and afflictions of the mind represented spiritual warfare between God and Satan. The insane weren't sick. They were possessed their bodies invaded by demons, their souls contested territory in a cosmic battle between good and evil.

This theological shift had profound consequences. If the mentally ill were possessed by demons, they became objects of fear and religious intervention rather than subjects of medical care. Exorcism became the primary treatment priests performing elaborate rituals to cast out demons through prayer, holy water, and increasingly through torture, on the

13

theory that making the body inhospitable would drive out the demon.

For those whose condition didn't respond to exorcism, which was most of them, the options were limited and grim. Many families locked insane relatives in cellars or attics, hidden from view. Others simply turned them out to wander. Medieval records describe "mad beggars" roaming from town to town, sleeping in fields, surviving on charity when they could get it.

Monasteries served as the era's closest equivalent to hospitals. Monks took seriously the Christian obligation to care for the suffering, and some monasteries maintained cells specifically for the insane. But these were more often dungeons than treatment facilities, underground rooms where the mad could be confined away from others, fed minimally, and prayed over in hopes of miraculous cure.

By the later Middle Ages, a new horror emerged: the witch trials. Between the 15th and 17th centuries, tens of thousands of people, mostly women, were executed for witchcraft. The Malleus Maleficarum (1487), the infamous witch-hunting manual, explicitly described symptoms of mental illness hearing voices, irrational beliefs, bizarre behavior as evidence of demonic possession requiring execution by fire.

Consider the case of Rebecca Nurse. In 1692, this 71-year-old woman in Salem, Massachusetts, was hanged as a witch. Her "symptoms" hearing voices, speaking to people who weren't there, bizarre behavior would today be recognized as late-onset schizophrenia or dementia. Thirty-nine people testified to her good character. She was executed anyway.

Many "witches" were almost certainly suffering from schizophrenia, psychotic depression, or manic episodes. They weren't possessed by demons or in league with Satan. They were sick. But medieval Europe burned them anyway.

Europe had forgotten what Greece and Rome knew, and what Jewish communities maintained: that the mentally ill weren't moral failures or demonic vessels but diseased patients requiring treatment.

THE ISLAMIC GOLDEN AGE: A DIFFERENT PATH (8TH–13TH CENTURIES CE)

While medieval Europe was burning mentally ill women as witches, the Islamic world was building psychiatric hospitals.

Beginning in the 8th century, major cities across the Islamic empire Baghdad, Cairo, Damascus, Aleppo, Fez— established bimaristans: hospitals that included dedicated wards for the mentally ill. These weren't warehouses or

15

prisons. The bimaristans represented a remarkably progressive approach as they were medical facilities based on a sophisticated understanding that mental illness was a disease requiring treatment.

The first psychiatric hospital opened in Baghdad in 705 CE. By the 10th century, the bimaristan in Baghdad had special wards for the insane, with separate facilities for men and women. Patients received regular meals, clean beds, and medical care. Physicians observed them carefully, adjusted treatments, and kept detailed records. The facility featured gardens, fountains, and courtyards, recognizing that pleasant environments aided recovery.

Islamic physicians made remarkable advances in understanding mental illness. Al-Razi (known in the West as Rhazes, 865–925 CE) wrote extensively about psychiatric conditions and their treatments. He distinguished between different types of mental disorders, melancholia, mania, and what he called "passive" versus "active" madness. He proposed that psychological trauma could cause illness. He advocated humane care and wrote: "The physician should give the patient hope even when danger signs are present, since the condition of the body is intertwined with the soul."

Ibn Sina (Avicenna, 980–1037 CE) wrote The Canon of Medicine, which became the standard medical text in both the Islamic world and later in Europe for centuries. He devoted significant sections to mental illness, describing symptoms, proposing causes, and recommending treatments. He understood that emotions and physical health were interconnected, that the mind could make the body sick, and vice versa. He noted that some mental illnesses were chronic and would require long-term management, while others were acute and potentially curable.

The bimaristans embodied this holistic approach. Patients lived in clean, well-ventilated buildings with gardens and fountains, architectural elements deliberately designed to provide therapeutic environments. They received regular meals, medication, and medical monitoring. Music therapy was standard the hospitals employed musicians who performed daily, having observed that music could calm agitated patients. Occupational therapy involved patients in meaningful work suited to their abilities gardening, craft work, and helping with hospital operations.

Treatment also included what we'd now call talk therapy. Islamic physicians conversed with patients to understand their troubles and gently challenge distorted thinking. They recognized that some mental disturbances arose from psychological conflicts or traumatic experiences, and that conversation could help resolve these issues.

Most importantly, Islamic hospitals treated the mentally ill with dignity. They weren't chained or displayed for entertainment. They weren't beaten or starved. They were patients receiving medical care, no different in kind from someone with a broken bone or fever.

A 10th-century text describes the necessity of confining actively psychotic patients "for their own protection and the protection of others," but emphasized that such confinement must be therapeutic, not punitive. Patients were to be treated with kindness, given opportunities for exercise and occupation, and released as soon as they were able to manage independently.

Why did the Islamic world achieve what Christian Europe couldn't during the same period? Islamic medicine was built on and extended Greco-Roman knowledge rather than rejecting it. Islamic theology didn't emphasize demonic possession the way Christianity did. The Quran mentions mental illness as a disease, not spiritual failure. And Islamic culture during this period valued learning and scientific inquiry, creating an intellectual environment where medical innovation could flourish.

Those bimaristans proved something important: even in the medieval world, with limited medical knowledge and no psychiatric medications, humane treatment of the severely mentally ill was possible. It required political will, cultural values supporting care over punishment, and adequate resources.

Europe wouldn't reach this level of sophistication in treating mental illness for another 600 years. The contrast is stark: same human condition, radically different responses. One civilization built hospitals. The other built pyres.

EARLY MODERN EUROPE: THE AGE OF REASON AND REVOLUTION (18TH–19TH CENTURIES)

Europe's reawakening to humane treatment came slowly, then suddenly.

By the 18th century, most European cities had institutions for the mentally ill, but "institution" is too generous a word. They were warehouses. London's Bethlem Royal Hospital ("Bedlam") was so notorious that citizens paid admission fees to watch the inmates as entertainment. Paris's Bicêtre and Salpêtrière hospitals confined thousands in conditions barely distinguishable from medieval dungeons.

Then in 1793, something changed. Philippe Pinel, physician-in-chief at the Bicêtre Hospital in Paris, made a decision that his colleagues considered insane: he removed the chains from fifty mentally ill patients who'd been shackled for years, some for decades.

This appeared simple, but it was revolutionary. For centuries, prevailing wisdom held that the mentally ill were dangerous animals requiring physical restraint. Chains weren't cruel; they were a necessity, or so everyone believed.

Pinel's colleagues warned that the unchained patients would become violent. Instead, many improved. Freed from restraints, treated with kindness, given clean quarters and regular meals, patients previously considered "incurable" became manageable. Some recovered enough to be discharged.

The experiment proved something crucial: humane treatment worked. It would take another half-century to translate that idea into systematic action.

And in America, one man believed he could design institutions that would embody these reform principles while avoiding the failures of Europe's asylums. His name was Thomas Story Kirkbride, and his vision would transform American psychiatry for better and for worse.

THE PATTERN REVEALED

This isn't ancient history. It's the reason I see the same symptoms on Los Angeles streets today that I evaluated in Ohio's locked wards fifty years ago. The pendulum swung but it never found center.

Humanity has psychiatrized what earlier eras demonized, but modern treatment isn't always more humane just more secular. The woman from the Prologue, arguing with invisible tormentors, shares something profound with Rebecca Nurse: both societies understood they were witnessing illness, but both chose abandonment over treatment.

The historical record reveals a consistent pattern: societies that acknowledge the reality of severe mental illness and accept collective responsibility for care find ways to provide it. Societies that deny this reality, fragment responsibility, or prioritize abstract principles over visible suffering produce the same outcome every time the mentally ill scattered to streets, jails, and early graves.

The lesson of five thousand years is not complicated: every society that has humanely managed severe mental illness has done so by assigning clear responsibility for care. Every society that has failed has done so by allowing that responsibility to be evaded. The Islamic bimaristans worked

21

because someone was responsible for every patient. Jewish communities maintained care across millennia because responsibility was embedded in law, not left to charity. The Kirkbride asylums, for all their eventual failures, began with the premise that the state accepted responsibility for those who could not care for themselves. What these systems shared was not resources, not medical knowledge, not cultural values but the simple principle that responsibility, once assigned, could not be escaped.

The question isn't whether the severely mentally ill exist. They always have. They always will. The question is what we're willing to do about it.

America once knew how to answer that question. In the mid-nineteenth century, reformers built a system that represented the best thinking of their era, institutions designed around the principle that environment itself could be therapeutic, that meaningful work restored dignity, that the mentally ill deserved sanctuary rather than punishment. That system was called the Kirkbride Plan, and understanding both its promise and its failure is essential to understanding where we are today.

That is where we turn next. The high-water mark of American psychiatric idealism came with a single man and a single architectural philosophy.

CHAPTER 2
THE KIRKBRIDE VISION

T he question hangs in the air from Chapter 1: If humanity has struggled with caring for the severely mentally ill for five thousand years, cycling through cruelty, compassion, and indifference, was there ever a moment when we got it right? A time when American society committed resources, will, and wisdom to actually helping the mentally ill recover?

The answer is complicated, but there was such a moment roughly from 1840 to 1880. For four decades, America built and operated psychiatric institutions that represented the best thinking of their era. They weren't perfect. They weren't a permanent solution. But they were something: a genuine attempt to treat mental illness as a medical disease requiring humane, therapeutic care.

This is the story of that moment and why it failed.

THE PROMISE: MORAL TREATMENT COMES TO AMERICA

By 1840, America's approach to mental illness was approaching crisis. The old colonial system families caring for their own, communities confining the troublesome in poorhouses or jails, had collapsed under the weight of urbanization and immigration. Cities were growing explosively, families were scattered, and too many severely mentally ill people were ending up in conditions that shocked even hardened observers.

But news of reforms in Europe was crossing the Atlantic. Philippe Pinel in France and William Tuke in England had demonstrated that "moral treatment," kindness, structure, therapeutic occupation, and humane conditions could help the mentally ill recover. Their institutions showed dramatically better outcomes than the traditional approach of chains, beatings, and confinement in filthy cells.

American reformers took notice. If moral treatment worked in small European institutions, perhaps it could work in America, but only if purpose-built facilities were created specifically for the task. The question was: who would champion such an expensive, politically difficult undertaking?

The answer came from an unlikely source: a forty-year-old former schoolteacher with no medical training, no political connections, and no money. But Dorothea Dix had something more powerful: moral clarity, relentless determination, and the ability to document suffering in ways that made it impossible to ignore.

DOROTHEA DIX: THE CRUSADER

Dorothea Lynde Dix was born in 1802 in Hampden, Maine, to an alcoholic father and a mentally ill mother. Her childhood was marked by poverty, neglect, and instability, experiences that would later fuel her lifelong advocacy for the vulnerable. She escaped her family at age twelve to live with her grandmother in Boston, where she received an education and eventually became a schoolteacher.

Dorothea Lynde Dix (1802–1887) was a pioneering advocate for the humane treatment of the mentally ill.

By 1841, Dix was thirty-nine years old, unmarried, and recovering from tuberculosis when a young theology student asked her to teach a Sunday school class at the East Cambridge jail. She agreed, expecting to teach scripture to prisoners. What she encountered there changed the trajectory of American psychiatry. The jail held mentally ill people who'd committed no crime. They were simply insane, and nowhere else would take them. Dix found them confined in unheated cells in the middle of a New England winter, chained to walls, left in their own waste. When she asked why they weren't given heat, the jailer explained with stunning casualness: "The insane don't feel cold the way normal people do."

Illustration representing the inhumane confinement endured by countless individuals with mental illness prior to 19th-century reforms.

DR. IVAN GULAS

Dix was horrified. But rather than simply express outrage, she did something more effective: she investigated. For two years, she traveled across Massachusetts, visiting every jail, poorhouse, and private "madhouse" she could find, documenting conditions with meticulous detail.

What she discovered was a pattern of systematic neglect and abuse that stretched across the state. Mentally ill people were "confined in cages, closets, cellars, stalls, pens! Chained, naked, beaten with rods, and lashed into obedience!" She found a woman who'd been kept in a cage in a poorhouse cellar for years. A man chained in a barn stall alongside livestock. Dozens more were living in conditions no animal should endure.

She documented specific cases with names, locations, and descriptions so precise that legislators couldn't dismiss them as exaggeration. In Danvers, she found a man confined in an unheated shed, naked, living in his own filth. In Saugus, a woman had been kept in a cage for years, never let out, fed through the bars like a zoo animal. In Groton, an elderly man was chained in a barn, his only contact with humans being when someone brought food once a day.

In January 1843, Dix presented a memorial to the Massachusetts legislature documenting what she'd found. The document was explosive, specific cases, named locations, and undeniable evidence:

"I proceed, gentlemen, briefly to call your attention to the present state of insane persons confined within this Commonwealth, in cages, closets, cellars, stalls, pens! Chained, naked, beaten with rods, and lashed into obedience! . . . I come to present the strong claims of suffering humanity. I come to place before the Legislature of Massachusetts the condition of the miserable, the desolate, the outcast."

The legislature was shocked. Politicians who'd happily ignored the mentally ill when they were out of sight couldn't ignore Dix's detailed testimony. Within months, Massachusetts appropriated funds to expand the Worcester State Hospital— one of the first state-funded psychiatric facilities in America.

But Dix wasn't finished. She'd found her calling, and she pursued it with the intensity of a religious mission. Over the next four decades, she traveled to every state and territory, documenting conditions, lobbying legislatures, and shaming politicians into action.

Her methodology was consistent: arrive in a state, spend months visiting every institution that housed the mentally ill, document conditions in meticulous detail, present findings to the legislature with specific recommendations, and refuse to leave until they acted. She personally visited over 300 jails and almshouses. She presented memorials to eighteen state legislatures. She lobbied Congress for federal funding, though that effort ultimately failed.

She traveled by stagecoach, steamboat, and horseback through regions with no roads, often in harsh weather, despite chronic health problems. She endured hostility from politicians who resented her interference, threats from institution administrators who didn't want their conditions exposed, and ridicule from newspapers that mocked a spinster woman presuming to tell men how to run government.

Her message was consistent and powerful: the insane are suffering needlessly. They deserve medical care, not punishment. They are sick, not criminal. The government has an obligation a moral obligation to provide humane treatment.

By the time of her death in 1887, Dix had been directly responsible for the founding or expansion of thirty-two mental hospitals across the United States and several more in Europe and Japan. Her crusade created the American asylum system. Whether that was ultimately good or bad depends on what happened next and on what would have happened without it.

But one thing is clear: the mentally ill in 1840 were living in cages and cellars, chained and beaten, dying in conditions of unimaginable cruelty. The new asylums, whatever their eventual flaws, had to be better than that.

The question was: what should these new institutions look like? How should they be designed to actually heal rather than simply warehouse? How could America avoid repeating the failures of European asylums, which too often became prisons rather than hospitals?

Thomas Story Kirkbride believed he had the answer.

THOMAS STORY KIRKBRIDE: THE MAN BEHIND THE PLAN

To understand why Kirkbride's institutions worked and why they eventually failed we need to understand the man himself. Thomas Story Kirkbride wasn't just an architect or administrator. He was a physician, a philosopher, a reformer, and in many ways, an idealist who believed that if you could just get the environment right, you could cure mental illness.

Born July 31, 1809, in Morrisville, Pennsylvania, Kirkbride grew up in a devout Quaker family. This upbringing shaped everything that followed. Quaker theology emphasized the "inner light" the belief that every human being possessed a divine spark and therefore deserved dignity and respect. This

31

applied even to especially to those societies considered broken or defective.

Dr. Thomas Story Kirkbride (1809–1883), whose principles of structure and environment shaped the design of nearly every major American asylum in the 19th century.

Quakers also believed in redemption through a proper environment. If sin resulted from bad influences, virtue could be cultivated through good ones. Apply this thinking to mental illness: perhaps madness resulted from bad environments urban squalor, family stress, moral corruption, and could be cured by placing patients in carefully designed therapeutic environments.

This wasn't mysticism. It was practical theology applied to medicine. And it would become the foundation of Kirkbride's entire career.

Kirkbride studied medicine at the University of Pennsylvania, graduating in 1832 at age twenty-three. He completed his medical training in Philadelphia during the cholera epidemic of 1832, working alongside physicians who were among America's medical elite. He saw firsthand how environment, sanitation, and systematic care could mean the difference between life and death.

The cholera epidemic taught Kirkbride crucial lessons. He observed that patients in cleaner, better-ventilated wards had better survival rates. He saw how organized, systematic care produced better outcomes than chaotic improvisation. He learned that environment mattered in ways that weren't immediately obvious but were nonetheless profound.

After graduation, he established a general medical practice in Philadelphia. He was a competent, respected physician who could have spent a comfortable career in private practice. But in 1840, he was invited to visit the Pennsylvania Hospital for the Insane as a consulting physician. What he saw there changed everything.

The Pennsylvania Hospital for the Insane, founded in 1841, was one of America's earliest psychiatric institutions. But "institution" gave it too much credit. When Kirkbride first walked through its doors in early 1840, he found conditions that would have shocked medieval observers.

Patients were confined in basement cells with stone floors and walls. No windows. No ventilation beyond small grates in heavy doors. No heat in winter except what seeped down from floors above. The cells were cleaned perhaps once a week sometimes less. The smell of human waste, unwashed bodies, and despair was overwhelming.

Violent patients were chained to walls or restrained in wooden cribs boxes that prevented any movement. One patient Kirkbride encountered, a man named William, had been in restraints for three years. His muscles had atrophied. He could barely walk, even when briefly released. His mind had deteriorated in the darkness and isolation until he was little more than an animal.

Kirkbride was appalled not just morally but medically. These conditions weren't treating mental illness they were causing it to worsen. Patients deteriorated in the darkness, isolation, and brutality. Anyone would go mad under such conditions, much less someone already struggling with psychological distress.

He wrote in his personal journal: "No physician who has seen what I have seen today could in good conscience allow this to continue. These are not criminals. They are sick human beings who deserve medical care. That they receive torture instead is a stain on our profession and our society."

When the hospital's board of managers asked him to become superintendent in 1841, he accepted immediately. He was thirty-one years old. He would hold that position for forty-two years, until his death in 1883. And he would spend those decades proving that another approach was possible.

THE KIRKBRIDE PHILOSOPHY: ARCHITECTURE AS MEDICINE

When Kirkbride became superintendent of the Pennsylvania Hospital for the Insane, he faced an overwhelming challenge. The physical plant was inadequate. The staff was untrained and often brutal. The patients were deteriorating. There was no established model for how a proper psychiatric hospital should operate.

He started with a radical premise: the building itself should be therapeutic. Not just a place where treatment happened, but an active agent of healing. If environment shaped character and behavior—as Quaker theology, his medical training, and his observations all suggested—then designing the right environment could actively promote recovery.

This wasn't a new idea Pinel and Tuke had emphasized humane environments but Kirkbride took it further. He believed you could systematize it, create architectural principles that would produce healing environments as reliably as proper surgical technique produced successful operations.

He began experimenting immediately at Pennsylvania Hospital. He opened windows to let in fresh air and sunlight. He moved patients out of basement cells into upper-floor rooms with natural light. He eliminated restraints except in cases of immediate danger. He required attendants to treat patients with respect and fired those who wouldn't.

The results were remarkable. Patients who'd been vegetative in dark cells improved when given light and human contact. Violent patients became calmer when treated with dignity instead of brutality. Those considered hopelessly insane began to show signs of awareness and responsiveness.

Kirkbride kept meticulous records of what worked and what didn't. He measured everything: patient outcomes by type of room, by amount of daily sunlight exposure, by type of occupation provided, by dietary changes. He was conducting what we'd now call empirical research, though he didn't use that terminology.

Over the next decade, working with architects and drawing on his observations, he developed a comprehensive plan. In 1854, he published On the Construction, Organization, and General Arrangements of Hospitals for the Insane a detailed manual that would become the blueprint for American psychiatric care.

KEY PRINCIPLES OF THE KIRKBRIDE PLAN

Kirkbride specified that asylums should be built on large tracts of land at least fifty acres, preferably one hundred or more. The location mattered: elevated ground with commanding views, away from the noise and vice of cities but close enough for family visits and supply access. The site should have good drainage, access to clean water, and soil suitable for farming.

The grounds should be carefully landscaped with gardens, orchards, walking paths, and therapeutic vistas. This wasn't just aesthetic preference. Kirkbride believed correctly, we now know that natural environments had therapeutic benefits. Modern research on biophilia and nature therapy has validated his intuition: patients who could walk through gardens, work with plants, or simply sit under trees showed better outcomes than those confined to urban institutions without green space.

The grounds should also be productive. Kirkbride's institutions typically included working farms where patients could engage in agricultural labor planting, harvesting, tending animals. This served multiple purposes: it reduced operating costs by producing food; it provided meaningful occupation that Kirkbride believed essential to recovery; it gave patients a sense of purpose and accomplishment; and it prepared patients for life after discharge, since farming skills were valuable in nineteenth-century America.

The Kirkbride Plan's most distinctive feature was its "bat-wing" or "shallow V" configuration. At the center stood the administration building, three or four stories tall, housing the superintendent's residence and offices. This placement was intentional: Kirkbride believed the superintendent should live at the facility, be available at all hours, and personally supervise all aspects of operation.

From this central building, patient wings extended backward at shallow angles, with each successive ward stepped back slightly from the one before. This created the characteristic bat-wing shape when viewed from above.

The genius of this design: every single patient room had windows on at least two sides often three. This provided cross-ventilation, crucial in an era before air conditioning, and guaranteed that no room was dark or airless. Even the deepest, most distant ward received abundant natural light and fresh air.

The wings were arranged hierarchically by patient condition. The most disturbed, violent, or deteriorated patients occupied rooms in the rear wings, furthest from the central administration building. These wards had the strongest construction and fewest privileges. As patients improved, they could be moved progressively forward toward the center. Each ward closer to the center offered better accommodations, larger windows, more privileges, and greater freedom.

The most improved patients lived in wards adjacent to the central building, with comfortable rooms, extensive privileges, and relative freedom to move about the grounds. This spatial progression embodied the asylum's therapeutic mission: movement from sickness toward recovery, from confinement toward freedom. Patients could literally see their progress reflected in their location within the building.

Kirkbride was obsessive, almost fanatical, about ventilation and light. This obsession saved lives.

He specified that each patient needed adequate air space, revolutionary in an era when most hospitals were cramped death traps where tuberculosis and typhoid spread unchecked. To achieve this, he required high ceilings, large windows that could be opened for fresh air, sophisticated ventilation systems that provided air circulation even in winter, and fireplaces or stoves in every ward for both heat and air circulation.

Every patient room had to have large windows at least one large window per bed, preferably more. Kirkbride believed that sunlight was therapeutic, that patients needed to see the changing seasons, and that views of nature aided recovery. Modern research has proven him right. Exposure to natural light regulates circadian rhythms, improves mood, provides Vitamin D, and aids healing. Studies of hospital patients show that those in rooms with windows facing natural views recover faster than those in rooms without views. Kirkbride knew this empirically 150 years before the research confirmed it.

The institutions also featured the most advanced sanitation systems available: running water throughout the building, bathrooms in every ward, modern sewage systems, steam heating, and regular cleaning protocols enforced by supervisors. This wasn't a humanitarian excess; it was a medical necessity. In the pre-antibiotic era, institutions were death traps if not properly maintained. Mortality rates in properly-run Kirkbride asylums were significantly lower than in older-style institutions.

A DAY IN THE LIFE: THE KIRKBRIDE ROUTINE

To truly understand how Kirkbride's system worked, we need to walk through a typical day at a well-run Kirkbride asylum in the 1870s. Let's follow "Sarah," a composite based on actual patient records from Pennsylvania Hospital.

Sarah is thirty-two years old, admitted three months ago with what Kirkbride would call "melancholia," what we'd now recognize as severe depression. She's been moved from the rear ward where she arrived to a middle ward a sign of progress.

6:00 AM: Attendants wake patients. Sarah's ward has twelve patients and two attendants. The attendants speak gently, helping patients who need assistance dressing. Sarah can dress herself but moves slowly, as depressed patients do.

6:30 AM: Breakfast in the ward dining room. The meal is simple but adequate: oatmeal, bread, butter, and coffee. Kirkbride specified dietary requirements carefully patients needed adequate nutrition to recover. Sarah eats little, but the attendant encourages her without forcing.

7:30 AM: Morning activities. Sarah is assigned to the sewing room. She works alongside other women from various wards, creating linens for the hospital under supervision. The work is simple but requires attention. Sarah makes mistakes, but the supervisor corrects her patiently.

10:00 AM: Break time. Patients have coffee and bread, can walk the ward corridors or sit in the common room. Sarah sits by a window, looking at the gardens outside. The attendant sits nearby, available if Sarah wants to talk.

10:30 AM: More work time or therapeutic activities. Today, Sarah's group goes to the garden to weed vegetable beds. It's spring, the work is light, the sun is warm. Sarah works slowly but works. Being outside, moving her body, doing something productive, this is the core of moral treatment.

12:00 PM: Dinner, the main meal. Roast beef, potatoes, carrots, bread, milk. The food is simple but wholesome. Patients eat in their ward dining room. Those who can do so serve themselves from communal platters a deliberate choice to maintain normal social skills.

1:00–3:00 PM: Rest period. Patients can nap, read, or pursue quiet activities. Sarah lies down but doesn't sleep—

depressed patients often can't. But the quiet time gives her mind rest from the morning's activities.

3:00 PM: Dr. Kirkbride makes his afternoon rounds. He visits every ward daily. He stops to speak with Sarah, briefly asks how she's feeling, whether she's eating, and how the sewing work is going. She answers in monosyllables, but she does answer. He notes her progress in his daily journal.

3:30–5:00 PM: Evening activities. Patients can attend a lecture (today: a talk on the solar system, with diagrams), participate in group singing, play parlor games, or simply socialize. Sarah sits in the back during the lecture, pays little attention, but she's present in a social setting—that's progress from the withdrawn isolation she showed on admission.

5:30 PM: Supper. A lighter meal: soup, bread, cheese, tea. Afterward, patients can walk the grounds if the weather permits. Sarah sits on a bench near the garden, watching the sunset. An attendant sits with her but doesn't force conversation.

7:00 PM: Evening reading hour. An attendant reads aloud from a popular novel while patients do handwork or simply listen. Sarah doesn't do handwork but listens. The story, something romantic and melodramatic, penetrates her depression slightly. She asks what happened to one of the characters. It's the first question she's initiated in weeks.

8:30 PM: Preparation for bed. Patients wash and change into nightclothes. The attendant helps those who need it.

9:00 PM: Lights out. Patients sleep in individual rooms; privacy was part of Kirkbride's plan. Sarah's room has a bed, a chair, a small table, and a window with a view of trees. It's plain but clean, with enough space to feel like a room rather than a cell. An attendant sits in the corridor outside, available if anyone needs help during the night.

This was the Kirkbride ideal: a structured day filled with meaningful activity, adequate rest, social interaction, medical supervision, and constant gentle encouragement toward normalcy.

Reconstructed depiction of a 19th-century Kirkbride ward.

Female dayroom at the Athens Lunatic Asylum, ca. late 19th century.

Not every patient improved. But many did. And even those who didn't improve felt human, treated with dignity, given purpose.

STAFF AND TRAINING: THE HUMAN ELEMENT

The Kirkbride Plan wasn't just about buildings and schedules. It was about the people, attendants, nurses, physicians, and administrators who made the system work.

Kirkbride understood something crucial: no architectural design could succeed without properly trained and motivated staff. He insisted on careful hiring, systematic training, and professional standards that were revolutionary for the era.

He personally interviewed every attendant candidate, looking for specific qualities: patience and gentleness, because the work required endless patience with patients who were repetitive, irrational, sometimes violent; physical strength combined with self-control, because attendants needed to restrain violent patients when necessary but controlled enough not to use force except as a last resort; literacy and basic education, because attendants had to keep detailed daily logs of patient behavior; and moral character, because he refused to hire anyone with a history of alcoholism or criminal behavior.

He paid above-market wages to attract better candidates. Attendees earned significantly more than factory workers, plus room and board. This was expensive but essential. You couldn't hire good people for bad wages.

Once hired, attendants underwent systematic training unprecedented in an era when most hospital workers learned by watching others. New attendants spent their first two weeks shadowing experienced ones, observing techniques for managing different patient behaviors. They learned to recognize signs of impending violence, methods for de-escalating agitation without restraints, and techniques for engaging withdrawn patients.

They attended weekly lectures by Kirkbride on mental illness its causes, manifestations, and treatment. This was remarkable: working-class attendants receiving medical education from a physician. Kirkbride believed that understanding mental illness helped attendants treat patients more humanely.

Most importantly, they learned Kirkbride's core principle: patients were sick people deserving respect, not criminals requiring punishment. Violence against patients, degrading language, neglect any of these meant immediate dismissal.

47

Kirkbride maintained quality through constant supervision. He personally visited every ward daily not just walking through, but stopping to observe attendants interacting with patients, asking questions, and checking records. He also solicited patient feedback, another innovation. He regularly asked patients privately how they were being treated. Complaints about specific attendants were investigated immediately. This created accountability, unusual for the era.

The system worked because Kirkbride combined high expectations with adequate support. He demanded professional behavior but provided the training, supervision, and compensation to achieve it. His asylum had remarkably low staff turnover, unusual in an era when most institutions churned through workers constantly.

THE SUCCESS YEARS: WHY IT SEEMED TO WORK

For roughly two decades (1850–1870), the Kirkbride system appeared to work remarkably well. Institutions following his plan reported recovery rates that seemed to validate his vision.

The Worcester State Hospital in Massachusetts one of the earliest and best-run Kirkbride asylum, reported in 1877 that of 1,841 patients admitted within three months of first symptoms, 1,080 (59%) were discharged as "recovered." Other institutions reported similar figures: New York's Bloomingdale

Asylum claimed a 58% recovery rate for recent cases. Pennsylvania's state hospitals reported 40–60% of patients improving enough to return home. Even chronic cases, those admitted after years of illness, showed 15–20% improvement rates.

These weren't random guesses. They were based on actual discharge records, follow-up with families, and careful documentation. Superintendents kept detailed statistics on admissions, treatments, outcomes, and subsequent reports on discharged patients. Modern analysis suggests these impressive numbers reflected several factors, some legitimate and some not.

First, diagnostic criteria were extremely broad, and many "patients" shouldn't have been institutionalized in the first place. Women were committed for "hysteria" or "moral insanity". Victorian-era terms for any behavior that challenged male authority. Men were committed for alcoholism, epilepsy, or simply being difficult. When these people were released after a few months, they were counted as "cured" even though they'd never had chronic mental illness.

Second, some patients did genuinely benefit from the structured, supportive environment. Someone experiencing their first psychotic break, given rest, good nutrition, removal from stress, and time to stabilize, might recover especially if their illness was triggered by temporary factors like fever, injury, or extreme stress. The moral treatment environment didn't cure schizophrenia, but it did help people whose breaks were acute rather than chronic.

Third, families often took patients back once the acute crisis had passed, whether or not they were truly "recovered." A daughter who'd been manic during the summer might be calmer by fall, calm enough that her family felt they could manage her at home. She was discharged as "improved" even though she'd likely have future episodes.

Fourth, the definition of "recovered" was generous. It often meant "able to function in society," not "completely symptom-free." A patient who was no longer actively psychotic or dangerous but still heard voices might be discharged as "recovered" if their family could manage them.

Even accounting for all these factors, something real was happening. The moral treatment environment, humane care, structured routine, meaningful occupation, and beautiful surroundings did help some people. Not everyone. Not permanently in many cases. But enough that Kirkbride's vision seemed vindicated.

Patients who'd been deteriorating in basement cells improved when given sunlight and human contact. Violent patients became calmer when treated with dignity instead of brutality. Withdrawn patients began to engage when given meaningful work and social interaction.

The question isn't whether Kirkbride asylums helped anyone; they clearly did. The question is whether they could scale sustainably, whether the model could work when demand exceeded capacity, and whether good intentions could survive economic and political pressures.

By 1880, nearly every state had at least one Kirkbride asylum. Seventy-three institutions were built to his exact specifications. Hundreds more borrowed elements of his design. American psychiatry had embraced his vision of architecture as medicine, environment as treatment.

And then it all started to fall apart.

THE SEEDS OF FAILURE

This chapter has traced the birth of American institutional psychiatry from Dorothea Dix's crusade through Thomas Kirkbride's revolutionary vision of architecture as medicine. For a brief shining moment, America built institutions that genuinely tried to heal rather than merely warehouse the mentally ill. The principles were sound: humane treatment, meaningful work, beautiful environments, trained staff, systematic care.

But even as Kirkbride's seventy-three asylums spread across the nation, the conditions for their failure were already present. The same forces that had overwhelmed European institutions would overwhelm American ones: too many patients, too few resources, too little political will to maintain what had been built. The idealism that created the Kirkbride system could not survive contact with the realities of funding, overcrowding, and chronic illness that doesn't respond to kindness alone.

One of the most faithful examples of Kirkbride's vision was built in Athens, Ohio, in 1874 the Athens Lunatic Asylum, designed by Kirkbride himself and constructed according to his exact specifications. It was meant to be a model of enlightened care, with 572 beds, sweeping grounds, and all the features Kirkbride believed would promote healing.

Athens Lunatic Asylum site plan (19th century).

The Administration Building of the Athens Lunatic Asylum in Athens, Ohio. The monumental centerpiece of this 19th-century Kirkbride-plan institution.

Nearly a century later, in 1971, I would walk through those same doors as a clinical psychology intern. What I found there and what had become of Kirkbride's noble vision is the subject of the next chapter.

CHAPTER 3
THE REALITY I FOUND

The smell hit first industrial disinfectant failing to mask decades of human despair. In the fall of 1971, I walked through the heavy doors of an Ohio state psychiatric hospital for the first time.

When this hospital opened in 1874, it was designed according to the revolutionary Kirkbride Plan. At its peak, the facility housed 1,800 patients across a sprawling 1,019-acre campus with 78 buildings. The self-sufficient complex included farms, dairy operations, orchards, and greenhouses, with patients participating in agricultural work as part of their therapy. The healing architecture had become the problem it was meant to solve.

WHAT WAS LOST

By 1880, the institution's 1,019 acres included 300 acres under cultivation, 100 head of cattle, 200 hogs, and extensive vegetable gardens producing 80% of its food needs. Patients who worked the farm weren't just passing time they were contributing to something real, seeing the results of their labor, experiencing the rhythm of seasons and growth that connected them to life outside their illness.

By 1971, the farm was gone. Sold off piece by piece as budgets tightened. The broad lawns where patients once played croquet had become parking lots. The greenhouses stood empty or demolished. What remained was a warehouse, not a therapeutic community. Patients who once might have found purpose tending tomatoes or feeding cattle now sat in hallways, staring at walls, with nothing to do but smoke cigarettes and wait for medication.

Kirkbride understood that human beings need purpose, that work itself is therapeutic, and that contributing to a community restores dignity that illness strips away. When the farms disappeared, so did any pretense that these institutions were about healing rather than containment.

THE DESCENT

By 1880, the institution was already operating above capacity. By 1900, the patient population had swelled to over 1,000. By the 1950s, it would house 1,800 patients in buildings designed for 572. The reasons were multiple: immigration brought millions to America; urbanization broke traditional family structures; courts sent psychiatric patients to asylums rather than jails; and most significantly, almost no one ever left.

The therapeutic ratio Kirkbride envisioned, one attendant for every eight patients, steadily deteriorated to one-to-thirty, then one-to-fifty. By World War II, some wards operated with ratios of 100:1. The beautiful grounds became parking lots and service roads. The therapeutic farm work became exploitative labor; patients provided free maintenance for an institution that couldn't function without them. A federal court wouldn't rule this practice unconstitutional until 1973.

The Great Depression devastated state mental hospital budgets precisely when demand soared as economically desperate families could no longer care for relatives at home. World War II delivered the death blow to any remaining pretense of therapeutic care. Young men were drafted, leaving hospitals critically understaffed. Patients were left in beds for days, developing bedsores. Violence became endemic as overwhelmed staff resorted to physical punishment to maintain any semblance of order.

On May 6, 1946, Life Magazine published "Bedlam 1946," exposing conditions at Pennsylvania's Byberry Hospital and Ohio's Cleveland State Hospital. The exposé was one of the first major investigative pieces to bring institutional conditions to mainstream public attention, and its impact was immediate and lasting.

The photographs shocked a nation still processing the recent liberation of Nazi concentration camps. The parallel was not lost on readers. Albert Maisel, the journalist who wrote the piece, explicitly invoked the comparison: "As I passed through some of Byberry's wards, I was reminded of the Nazi concentration camps at Belsen and Buchenwald." The comparison was inflammatory, but Maisel had chosen it deliberately. He wanted Americans to confront an uncomfortable truth: that conditions in their own institutions, housing their own citizens, had descended to a level that evoked humanity's darkest recent chapter.

Representative illustration of conditions similar to those described in
LIFE Magazine's 1946 "Bedlam" report. Because the original
photographs are not in the public domain, this image serves as a
historically informed depiction of the overcrowding and severe neglect
prevalent in state psychiatric hospitals of the period.

Was the comparison fair? The state hospitals were not death camps. There was no program of deliberate extermination. The patients were not being murdered; they were being neglected. But Maisel's point that the visual and moral parallels were undeniable, that democratic America had created conditions this degrading struck with the force he intended. The images of American citizens, naked, emaciated, huddled against walls, forced a reckoning that changed public perception of institutional psychiatry forever.

The exposé led to investigations, reforms, and increased funding. But the structural problems remained: too many patients, too few staff, too little money, and no sustainable model for providing genuine treatment to populations this large. What I witnessed twenty-five years later showed that, despite reforms, the fundamental warehousing of human beings continued. The system had been patched but not transformed.

WHAT I FOUND

The facility, perched on its hilltop overlooking the Hocking River Valley, still commanded an imposing presence against the Ohio sky. To reach the locked wards, I knocked and waited, sometimes for five minutes for an overworked attendant managing forty or fifty patients alone. The door would close behind me with that heavy click of the lock engaging. That sound was a daily reminder: these people had surrendered their freedom, often decades ago.

The central administration building of the Athens State Hospital (formerly the Athens Lunatic Asylum), photographed in the early 1900s.

Aerial view of the Athens Lunatic Asylum (Athens State Hospital), illustrating the characteristic staggered-wing "Kirkbride Plan" design intended to maximize light, ventilation, and therapeutic space.

The hallways stretched like tunnels through time. Patients lined the corridors, some sitting on cold linoleum, mechanically smoking, others pacing endless circuits, still others frozen in catatonic postures that defied comfort. Many

60

had been here twenty, thirty, even forty years. They'd become ghosts haunting their own lives, forgotten by families, attended by staff who could barely distribute medications on schedule.

THE STAFF I ENCOUNTERED

As a psychology intern, my job was to conduct mental status examinations on the locked wards, systematic assessments of orientation, memory, cognition, and psychiatric symptoms. Each examination was a window into a mind struggling against its own dysfunction.

The patients I examined bore the unmistakable marks of long institutionalization. Their fingers were stained yellow-brown from decades of smoking cigarettes, which was universal on the wards, one of the few pleasures permitted, and the acrid smell of tobacco permeated every corridor. Many walked with what staff called the "Thorazine shuffle," a slow, stiff, flat-footed gait caused by the antipsychotic medications that had replaced restraints as the primary means of control.

The orientation questions revealed the depth of disconnection. "What year is it?" I would ask. One man, admitted in the 1950s, answered "1953" without hesitation, the last year that had meant anything to him, the last year he had participated in the world beyond these walls. He wasn't

61

confused about the passage of time; time had simply stopped mattering.

One woman exhibited classic catatonic features waxy flexibility, where her limbs would remain in whatever position I placed them, frozen like a mannequin being posed. She could hold her arm extended for minutes, perfectly still, in a position that would exhaust a healthy person in seconds. Her eyes tracked movement, suggesting consciousness, but she made no voluntary movements of her own.

Many patients had developed what I came to think of as an institutional gait, a shuffling, purposeless movement up and down the corridors that was less walking than a form of self-stimulation, the body's attempt to create meaning through motion when meaning had been stripped away. They paced the same routes, day after day, wearing subtle paths in the linoleum.

The burn holes in shirts and pants told their own story. Cigarettes dropped by patients too sedated or too psychotic to manage them safely had scorched fabric, sometimes skin. The burns were treated, the cigarettes were not taken away, small comforts were too few to eliminate, even dangerous ones.

What struck me most forcefully was how the ward itself had imprinted on these patients. After decades in the same environment, following the same routines, eating the same food, seeing the same faces, they had become institutional creatures. The institution hadn't cured them; it had become them.

It is with some embarrassment that I now admit that the very first thing I did when I got home each day was to take a shower and change clothes. The smell of the wards' disinfectant and cigarette smoke and something else, something human and despairing that I could never quite name clung to fabric and hair. I now think that I was also trying to wash off the weight of what I had witnessed.

THE CEMETERIES

The asylum's three cemeteries contained nearly 1,930 graves. Many were marked only with numbers rather than names. Not because the hospital didn't know who was buried there, they kept meticulous records, but because no one came to claim the bodies. No family wanted their name associated with a relative who had died in a lunatic asylum. The numbered markers weren't administrative convenience; they were monuments to shame.

Numbered grave markers in the asylum cemetery at Athens, Ohio, where patients were buried without names, identified only by numbers rather than identities.

Families didn't just commit troublesome relatives, they erased them. Once someone entered an asylum, they often ceased to exist for their families. Visits dwindled, then stopped. Letters went unanswered. When patients died after decades of institutionalization, there was no one left who remembered them, no one who would pay for a headstone.

I think of those numbered graves whenever I hear people speak of the mentally ill as problems to be managed rather than people to be helped. The stigma that filled those cemeteries with nameless dead hasn't disappeared. It has simply moved from asylum grounds to city sidewalks.

THE LOBOTOMY CATASTROPHE

But what haunts me most are the lobotomy patients.

In the 1930s, Portuguese neurologist António Egas Moniz proposed that certain mental illnesses were caused by abnormal patterns of neural activity, which he called "pathological circuits" that became fixed in the brain's prefrontal regions. The solution, Moniz reasoned, was surgical: sever the connections that maintained these pathological loops, and the symptoms would cease. He won the 1949 Nobel Prize in Medicine for this work.

From a modern perspective, Moniz was not wrong that the prefrontal cortex plays a central role in emotional regulation, planning, and self-control. He was catastrophically wrong about what happens when you destroy it.

What drove institutions to embrace lobotomy was desperation. In the 1930s and 1940s, there were no antipsychotic medications, no mood stabilizers, no antidepressants. The only tools available were restraints, hydrotherapy, insulin shock, electroconvulsive therapy, and even these offered limited relief for the severely ill. Meanwhile, state hospitals were drowning. Wards designed for hundreds held thousands. Violent patients overwhelmed the staff. Families begged for any intervention that might help.

Into this void stepped Walter Freeman. Freeman transformed Moniz's careful surgical approach into an assembly-line procedure. His innovation the transorbital lobotomy, required no operating room, no anesthesia beyond electroshock, no neurosurgical training. An instrument resembling an ice pick, inserted through the eye socket, tapped through the thin bone with a hammer, swept back and forth to sever frontal connections. The procedure took ten minutes. Freeman could perform dozens in a day.

Freeman's first transorbital lobotomy used an actual ice pick from his kitchen. He performed it on January 17, 1946, in his Washington, D.C. office on a 29-year-old housewife. After rendering her unconscious through electroshock, he inserted the ice pick above her eyeball, hammered it through the orbital bone into her brain, swept it back and forth, then repeated the procedure through the opposite eye. When he was done, he sent her home in a taxi.

The appeal to overwhelmed institutions was obvious. A lobotomy costs $250; maintaining a patient in a state hospital costs $35,000 per year. Freeman traveled the country in what he called his "lobotomobile," performing over 3,400 lobotomies in his career. His patients ranged from age four to their eighties.

This hospital performed lobotomies from 1947 to 1954 approximately 200 irreversible brain surgeries. The archives document that Freeman himself performed lobotomies here during the 1950s, sometimes more than twenty in a single day.

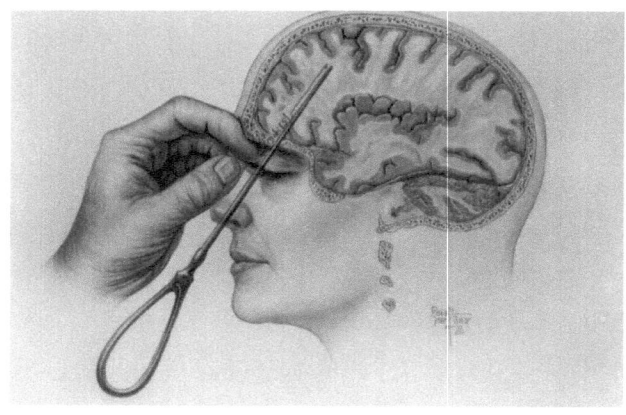

A needle placed above the eye penetrates to the frontal lobe

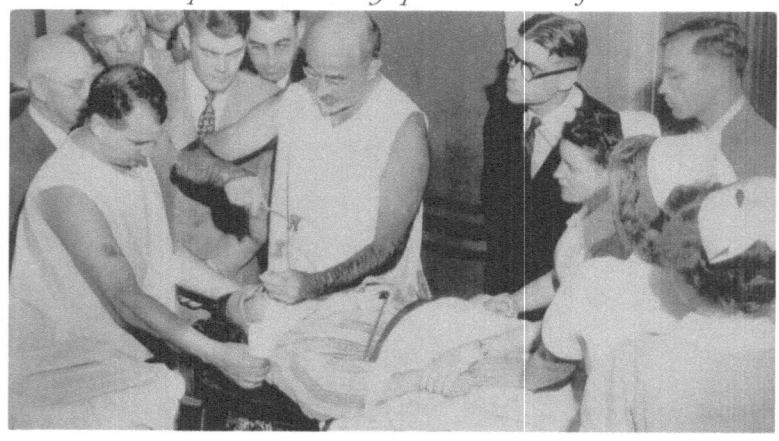

Dr. Walter Freeman performing a transorbital lobotomy, c. 1940s.
Source: National Library of Medicine, public domain.

I saw Freeman's handiwork firsthand in those wards. The lobotomized patients moved through the halls like the walking dead. Their faces were masks of blankness, devoid of the animation that defines human consciousness. One woman, lobotomized in 1952 for "agitated depression," spent her days arranging and rearranging three objects on her nightstand a comb, a photograph, and a plastic flower. When asked about her life before, she would smile vaguely and say nothing.

Another patient, a man in his forties lobotomized for "aggressive behavior," sat in the same chair every day, staring at nothing. He could follow simple commands, stand up, sit down, and eat your meal, but initiated nothing. The surgery had removed not just his aggression but his humanity.

The scars were subtle but unmistakable once you knew what to look for: small indentations above the eyes where the instrument had entered, a certain deadness in the gaze, a quality of absence that went beyond psychiatric symptoms. These weren't patients who were withdrawn or catatonic from illness they were people whose essential selves had been surgically removed.

What the theory failed to account for was that the frontal lobes are not merely processors of emotion; they are the integrative heart of human life. They enable us to plan for the future, to weigh consequences, to feel empathy, to pursue goals. They are, in a very real sense, where personhood resides. To damage them is to damage the very essence of what makes someone who they are.

Freeman believed he was curing mental illness. His definition of success was the absence of troublesome behavior, not the restoration of personhood. A lobotomized patient who sat quietly and caused no problems was considered a success, even if they could no longer feel joy, form relationships, or engage with life.

Approximately 490 of Freeman's patients died from the procedure a mortality rate of about 14 percent. He performed his last lobotomy in 1967; his final patient died of cerebral hemorrhage during the procedure. By then, approximately 40,000 Americans had undergone the surgery. The patients I saw in 1971 were the survivors, if survival is the right word for what remained of them.

THE THORAZINE REVOLUTION

By 1971, antipsychotic medication had transformed institutional life. Thorazine and similar drugs had replaced restraints and lobotomies as the primary means of managing severe mental illness. Patients lined up twice daily for their doses, and wards that once required physical control now functioned with chemical control.

The medications were a genuine advance; they reduced suffering, made treatment possible, and offered hope where there had been none. But they also created dangerous illusions. Policymakers saw calm patients and concluded they no longer needed institutional care. They didn't understand that the calm depended on supervised medication, that most patients would stop taking pills once discharged, and that the underlying illness remained untouched.

THE OLD EXTREME: WHEN COMMITMENT WAS TOO EASY

For most of American history, getting someone committed to a psychiatric hospital was frighteningly easy, and the system's abuses were indefensible.

Elizabeth Packard's story captures the system's casual cruelty. In 1860, Illinois law explicitly allowed husbands to commit their wives to asylums without evidence of mental illness and without any hearing. Packard, an intelligent woman in her forties, disagreed with her husband on matters of religion and women's rights. He had her forcibly taken to Jacksonville State Hospital. For three years, she was locked in an asylum, not because she was mentally ill, but because her husband found her opinions objectionable and the law gave him absolute power over her freedom.

The pattern repeated across demographic groups. Women were routinely committed for "hysteria" or "moral insanity," Victorian-era terms for any behavior that challenged male authority. Immigrants made up half of New York's institutionalized population by 1912, often committed for cultural behaviors rather than genuine mental illness.

The reasons people were committed read like a catalog of absurdity: menstrual derangements, postpartum depression, masturbation, epilepsy, novel reading, disappointed love, religious enthusiasm, laziness, and imaginary female trouble. The commitment process itself was perfunctory two doctors' signatures, a judge's rubber stamp, confined indefinitely. No lawyer, no hearing, no meaningful appeal. By 1955, this system had institutionalized 558,922 Americans.

Published by STEAKLY & LULLAY, Blank Book Manufacturers and Legal Blank Publishers, Opera House Building, Columbus, O. 185

INQUEST.
Revised Statutes, Secs. 706-715.

Before *Newell Corner* _____ Probate Judge.

Morgan _____ County, Ohio.

Office of Probate Judge,

McConnelsville Ohio, *November 15* 1884

INQUEST OF LUNACY.

In the matter of *Sarah Miller* _____ an alleged insane person.

This day this cause came on to be heard by me, *Newell Corner*

Probate Judge of *Morgan* _____ County, Ohio, at my office in the _____ in said County, at the hour of *2* o'clock *P* M.

Present *Sarah Miller* _____ the patient; and having *heard the testimony of J E Brown*
M Jenkins Barns and others

I do find that the said *Sarah Miller* is insane; that she has a legal settlement in *Windsor* Township in said County; that she has been an inhabitant of the State of Ohio for one year last past; that her insanity has occurred during the time that she has resided in this State; that her being at large is dangerous to the safety of the community; that she is a fit subject to be sent to the Asylum for the Insane to undergo treatment therein. And that she is entitled to admission into the Asylum for the Insane of the State of Ohio, at *Athens Ohio*

Newell Corner

Probate Judge *Morgan* County, Ohio.

The State of Ohio, *Morgan* County, ss.

I, *Newell Corner* _____ Probate Judge of said County, do hereby certify that the above is a full and true copy of my findings in said cause.

In Witness Whereof, I have hereunto subscribed my name and affixed the seal of said Court, at *McConnelsville*, Ohio, this *15th* day of *November* 1884

Newell Corner

Probate Judge.

Inquest of Lunacy, Morgan County, Ohio (1884). This document, preserved in the patient records of the Athens Lunatic Asylum, reflects the legal process by which individuals were declared "insane" and committed to the institution.

The State of Ohio, Muskingum County, ss.

Probate Court,

Zanesville, July 9th, 1874

IN THE MATTER OF

Eliza Day

INQUEST OF LUNACY.

Be it Remembered, That on the 7th day of July, 1874, application was made to the Court, in due form of law, for the admission of Eliza Day into the " Athens Ohio Lunatic Asylum" as a State patient; and an affidavit, in manner and form as prescribed by the Statute, was filed; thereupon a warrant was issued, and on the 9th day of July 1874 the patient was brought before the Court; W. C. Earhart M. D., a respectable physician of this County, and John H. Pilana, O. Knapp, George H. Clow and Robert Day were sworn and examined as witnesses; and the Court having heard all the testimony, and held the inquest as provided by law, and being fully advised in the premises, do find that the said Eliza Day is insane, that her insanity is of less than two years' duration, and being at large, is dangerous to the community. The Court do further find that she has a legal settlement in Blue rock, township in this County, and that she is, and was, at the time her insanity occurred, a resident of the State of Ohio.

It is Therefore Ordered, by the Court that W. C. Earhart the medical witness herein, make out a certificate of this case according to law, and file the same in this Court; and it is further Ordered, that a copy of said certificate, together with a copy of this finding of the Court, be transmitted to the Superintendent of the " Athens Ohio Lunatic Asylum," and this cause is continued.

J. H. Morgan, PROBATE JUDGE.

Inquest of Lunacy, Muskingum County, Ohio (1875). This commitment order authorized the transfer of a patient to the Ohio Lunatic Asylum. Preserved in the historical patient records associated with the Athens Lunatic Asylum.

The abuses were indefensible. Something had to change. The question was whether the pendulum would find a reasonable center or swing violently to the opposite extreme.

By 1971, the American psychiatric hospital had traveled an extraordinary distance from Kirkbride's vision. The therapeutic community had become a warehouse. The healing architecture had become a prison. The moral treatment had become chemical sedation.

The patients I evaluated were living in the ruins of a broken promise. President Kennedy had declared war on these institutions in 1963, envisioning a network of community mental health centers that would render the old asylums unnecessary. The vision was humane, modern, and optimistic. But Kennedy was assassinated weeks after signing the legislation, and what followed was not transformation but abandonment. The hospitals emptied; the alternatives never appeared. What I saw in Ohio was the wreckage a system dismantling itself with no plan for what came next. Understanding how we arrived at this catastrophe requires us to return to Kennedy's promise, to the personal tragedy that may have shaped it, and to the forces that ensured it would never be kept.

CHAPTER 4
THE KENNEDY VISION

FEBRUARY 5, 1963: A HISTORIC MESSAGE

The members of Congress who gathered to hear President John F. Kennedy's special message on February 5, 1963, had no idea they were witnessing history. No American president had ever devoted an entire address to mental illness. The topic was considered shameful, something families whispered about but never discussed publicly. Mental hospitals were places people disappeared into, not subjects for presidential oratory.

Kennedy changed that in a single morning.

"I propose a national mental health program," he declared, "to assist in the inauguration of a wholly new emphasis and approach to care for the mentally ill. This approach relies primarily upon the new knowledge and new drugs acquired and developed in recent years, which make it possible for most of the mentally ill to be successfully and quickly treated in their own communities and returned to a useful place in society."

The words were carefully chosen, but Kennedy's delivery carried unusual emotion. Aides who had worked on dozens of presidential speeches noticed something different in his voice that day a personal intensity that went beyond political calculation. What they could not know was that Kennedy's passion for this cause likely stemmed from genuine compassion shaped by family tragedy compassion that would prove both noble in intent and naïve about the consequences of the reforms it would inspire.

He called the state hospital system a "cold mercy" and a "shameful" burden on American ideals. He spoke of patients "abandoned" in "institutional purgatory" under conditions that would "appall the conscience" if they were more widely known. The language was startling in its moral force. Presidents spoke this way about foreign tyranny, not about American institutions.

"We must act," Kennedy urged Congress and the nation, "to end that abandonment, mistreatment and institutional purgatory which has too long been the lot of the mentally ill."

His vision was ambitious in scope. He proposed federal funding to build 1,500 community mental health centers across America, each serving a catchment area of

75,000 to 200,000 people. These centers would provide a comprehensive array of services: outpatient treatment, emergency psychiatric services, partial hospitalization for those who needed daytime care but could return home at night, short-term inpatient care for acute episodes, and consultation services to schools, courts, and community agencies.

No American would be more than an hour's drive from comprehensive mental health care. The massive state hospitals those sprawling institutions that had become warehouses of despair would gradually empty as patients received treatment in their own communities. Eventually, Kennedy promised, the old asylums would close entirely, relics of a more barbaric age.

It was a beautiful vision. But what drove this passion? Why did a president facing the Cold War, the civil rights crisis, and a thousand other demands choose to spend political capital on an issue most Americans preferred to ignore?

The answer may lie in a closely guarded family secret a personal tragedy that likely haunted John F. Kennedy every day of his presidency.

THE FAMILY SECRET: ROSEMARY KENNEDY

To understand what may have driven Kennedy's commitment to mental health reform, we must go back more than two decades, to a decision made in secret that destroyed a young woman's life and scarred a family forever.

Rose Marie Kennedy, called Rosemary by her family, was born on September 13, 1918, the third child and first daughter of Joseph P. Kennedy Sr. and Rose Fitzgerald Kennedy. From the beginning, something was different about her. She was slower to crawl, slower to walk, and slower to speak than her older brothers, Joe Jr. and John. The family later attributed this to a traumatic birth; the obstetrician had been delayed, and a nurse allegedly held the baby in the birth canal for two hours, potentially depriving her brain of oxygen.

Whatever the cause, Rosemary struggled in ways her siblings did not. She had difficulty with reading and arithmetic. Her handwriting remained childlike. She couldn't keep up with the competitive Kennedy clan in their fierce games of touch football and sailing races. In a family that prized achievement above all else, Rosemary was perpetually behind.

But "behind" is not the same as incapable. Rosemary learned to read and write. She kept a diary, recording her daily activities in simple but coherent prose. She attended special schools, to be sure, but schools nonetheless. She traveled with her family to England when her father was appointed Ambassador to the Court of St. James in 1938. She was presented to King George VI and Queen Elizabeth at Buckingham Palace, wearing a white gown and executing the required curtsy without incident. Photographs from the period show a beautiful young woman, elegantly dressed, smiling alongside her glamorous sisters.

Rosemary Kennedy, 1938. Photograph: John F. Kennedy Presidential Library and Museum (public domain).

By modern standards, Rosemary would likely be classified as having mild intellectual disability perhaps an IQ in the 70s or low 80s. She was not severely impaired. She was not psychotic. She was simply slower than her extraordinarily accomplished siblings, a young woman who needed patience and support rather than the relentless pressure to excel that defined Kennedy family life.

By her early twenties, however, Rosemary's behavior began to change in ways that alarmed her father. She had mood swings and periods of agitation followed by dark withdrawals. She may have experienced seizures. Most troubling to Joe Kennedy, she showed interest in men and sexuality. She would sometimes sneak out at night from the convent school where she boarded. There were fears, never confirmed, that she might become pregnant, bringing scandal upon a family with towering political ambitions.

Joe Kennedy was building a dynasty. His eldest son, Joe Jr., was being groomed for the presidency. John was already showing political promise. The last thing the family needed was a scandalous daughter whose behavior couldn't be controlled a daughter who might say the wrong thing to the wrong person, who might embarrass them on the public stage they were so carefully constructing.

Rose Kennedy, a devout Catholic, would never have considered institutionalization for her daughter. She believed in prayer, in patience, in accepting God's will. But in 1941, Joe

Kennedy learned of a new procedure that promised to solve difficult cases like Rosemary's. A simple operation, doctors told him, that could calm her mood swings, stop her wandering, and make her more manageable. The procedure was called a prefrontal lobotomy.

The doctors who would perform the procedure were Walter Freeman and James Watts, the same men whose assembly-line lobotomies would devastate patients at Athens State Hospital and dozens of other institutions across America.

Freeman was evangelical about the lobotomy's potential. He had performed dozens of the procedures and reported remarkable results: violent patients became docile, agitated patients became calm, and difficult patients became manageable. He downplayed the risks and side effects, dismissing concerns about personality changes as minor trade-offs for behavioral improvement.

What Freeman didn't tell Joe Kennedy, what he may not have fully acknowledged even to himself, was that the procedure was still experimental, its long-term effects unknown. He didn't mention that some patients emerged as emotional zombies, stripped of personality and initiative. He didn't explain that the procedure was irreversible, that whatever was cut could never be reconnected.

Joe Kennedy decided without consulting his wife or his other children. Rose was told only that Rosemary was going to have an operation that would help her. She wasn't told what kind of operation. She wasn't given the opportunity to object.

In November 1941, Rosemary Kennedy, age 23, was taken to George Washington University Hospital in Washington, D.C. She was not told what was about to happen to her.

What occurred in that operating room would haunt the Kennedy family for generations.

Freeman and Watts used a procedure called prefrontal leucotomy. With Rosemary awake, the brain has no pain receptors, so only local anesthesia was needed for the scalp incision. They drilled two small holes in her skull, one on each side. Through these holes, they inserted a spatula-like instrument called a leucotome.

Freeman later described his technique: he would have the patient perform simple tasks, counting backward, reciting the Lord's Prayer, singing a song while he cut. He would sever the white matter connecting the prefrontal cortex to the rest of the brain, slicing through neural pathways while monitoring the patient's responses. When the patient became incoherent or confused, he knew he had cut enough.

With Rosemary, they cut too much.

The young woman who had danced with royalty, who had kept a diary, who had traveled the world with her family, emerged from the operating room essentially destroyed. Her mental capacity regressed to that of a two-year-old. She could no longer walk properly, requiring assistance for the rest of her life. Her speech became unintelligible, garbled sounds rather than words. She was incontinent. The vibrant, if challenged, young woman was gone. In her place was someone who would require total care for the remaining sixty-three years of her life.

Joe Kennedy's response to this catastrophe was not grief or guilt but concealment. He could not admit what he had done could not acknowledge that his decision had destroyed his daughter. So he made her disappear.

Rosemary was sent to Craig House, a private psychiatric facility in New York, and later to St. Coletta School for Exceptional Children in Jefferson, Wisconsin a Catholic institution far from the family's East Coast power base. She would live there for the rest of her life, until her death in 2005 at age 86.

Rose Kennedy was told that Rosemary had gone away to a special school where she was making progress. She was not told about the lobotomy. She was not told that her daughter could no longer walk or speak. For twenty years, Rose Kennedy did not know what had happened to her child. She did not visit. She was not allowed to visit.

The other Kennedy children were told even less. When they asked about Rosemary, they were told she was "away," or "doing fine," or "happy where she is." The subject was closed. In a family that discussed everything around the dinner table, politics, history, and current events, Rosemary became the one topic that was forbidden.

John F. Kennedy was 24 years old when his sister was lobotomized. He was serving in the Navy, soon to become a war hero in the Pacific. Did he know what his father had done? Almost certainly, he learned the truth eventually, family secrets have a way of emerging. But he never spoke of it publicly, never acknowledged what had happened to his sister.

Rose Kennedy finally learned the truth in the early 1960s, when John was president. The circumstances of her discovery are unclear perhaps another family member finally told her, perhaps she simply demanded answers after two decades of evasion. What is known is that she was devastated.

She began visiting Rosemary at St. Coletta's, making regular trips to Wisconsin that she had never made before. She found her daughter profoundly disabled but still, somehow, present, still capable of recognizing family members, still able to express emotion even if she couldn't express words. Rose would later write about these visits, about the sorrow of seeing what her daughter had become, about her own guilt for not protecting her.

Joe Kennedy, by this point, had suffered a massive stroke that left him unable to speak. He could not explain himself, could not apologize, could not ask forgiveness. He died in 1969, having never publicly acknowledged what he had done to his daughter.

Did Rosemary's fate influence John F. Kennedy's passionate commitment to mental health reform? Historians cannot say with certainty. Kennedy never publicly acknowledged the lobotomy. The family's secrecy was absolute.

But the circumstantial evidence is compelling.

Kennedy's passion for mental health reform was unusual and unprecedented for an American president. His language about institutional abuse was personal and emotional in ways his other policy speeches were not. He spoke of patients "abandoned" and "mistreated" in "institutional purgatory" with an intensity that seemed to come from somewhere deeper than policy briefings.

If Kennedy knew what Freeman had done to Rosemary and it seems likely he did then he had witnessed institutional psychiatry at its worst. He had seen a system that enabled doctors like Freeman, that provided them with patients, that allowed assembly-line brain surgery without meaningful oversight. He had seen a family destroyed by a procedure performed in the name of making a "difficult" person more "manageable."

Perhaps, in championing mental health reform, Kennedy was seeking redemption for what his family had done. Perhaps he was trying to ensure that no other family would suffer as his had suffered. Perhaps he simply understood, in a way that most politicians could not, how badly the system was broken.

What historians can say with certainty is that the Kennedy who stood before Congress on February 5, 1963, calling for an end to "institutional purgatory," had personal knowledge of what that purgatory looked like. His sister was still living it.

The problem was that Kennedy's response, if indeed influenced by Rosemary, contained a fatal error in reasoning. Because institutions had enabled Freeman, because institutional psychiatry had destroyed his sister, the institutions themselves must be eliminated. The alternative, fixing them, funding them adequately, regulating them properly, ensuring that procedures like lobotomy could never again be performed without oversight, was apparently never seriously considered. It was an understandable error. It was also a catastrophic one.

EUNICE'S CRUSADE

If John Kennedy's response to Rosemary's fate was legislative reform, his sister Eunice Kennedy Shriver's response was even more direct.

Eunice, five years younger than Rosemary, had been close to her older sister growing up. She had witnessed Rosemary's struggles, had seen how the family's competitive culture left her sister perpetually behind. After learning the truth about the lobotomy, Eunice channeled her grief and anger into action.

In 1962, Eunice published an article in the Saturday Evening Post that broke decades of Kennedy family silence. Though she did not mention the lobotomy, she acknowledged publicly for the first time that Rosemary was intellectually disabled. "Early in life, Rosemary was different," she wrote. "She was slower to crawl, slower to walk and speak than her two bright brothers." The article was remarkable for its candor in an era when families hid disabled children from public view.

But Eunice didn't stop at confession. She dedicated her life to transforming how American society treated people with intellectual disabilities. In 1968, she founded the Special Olympics, initially as a summer camp for children with disabilities at her home in Maryland. The organization grew into an international movement that has served millions of athletes worldwide.

The Special Olympics embodied a philosophy that was the opposite of what had been done to Rosemary: instead of trying to "fix" people with disabilities through surgery, it celebrated their abilities. Instead of hiding them away in institutions, it put them on playing fields before cheering crowds. Instead of treating them as problems to be managed, it recognized them as people with potential.

Eunice Kennedy Shriver passed away on August 11, 2009, four years after her sister Rosemary. By then, the Special Olympics had spread to 170 countries, and the stigma around intellectual disability that had led to Rosemary's lobotomy had been transformed in no small part because of Eunice's work.

THE COMMUNITY MENTAL HEALTH ACT OF 1963

While personal tragedy may have driven Kennedy's passion, translating that passion into legislation required the work of policy experts and bureaucrats who had been laboring in obscurity for years.

The chief architect of the Community Mental Health Centers Act was Dr. Robert Felix, director of the National Institute of Mental Health since its founding in 1949. Felix had been advocating for community-based mental health care for more than a decade, and Kennedy's election finally gave him a president who would listen.

Felix believed that the state hospital system was fundamentally flawed, not just underfunded but conceptually wrong. Isolating mentally ill people in distant institutions, he argued, cut them off from the community connections essential to recovery. Better to treat people in their own neighborhoods, close to family and friends, maintaining the social ties that give life meaning.

His vision was comprehensive. The community mental health centers wouldn't just provide outpatient therapy, they would serve as hubs for prevention, education, and early intervention. They would work with schools to identify children at risk. They would train community members to

89

recognize mental health crises. They would coordinate with police, courts, and social services to keep people out of hospitals in the first place.

Felix testified before Congress with evangelical fervor. "Within a decade or two," he predicted, "state mental hospitals as we know them will cease to exist." The old asylums would become obsolete, replaced by a network of community centers that would treat mental illness before it became severe enough to require institutionalization.

It was a beautiful vision. It was also dangerously naive.

The Community Mental Health Centers Act was passed by Congress in October 1963 with broad bipartisan support. It authorized $150 million over three years for construction grants federal money to build the physical facilities that would house the new system.

Official U.S. government photograph of a bill-signing ceremony at the White House, mid-20th century. Public domain.

But there was a fatal flaw buried in the legislation, a flaw that would doom the entire enterprise.

The Act funded construction but not operations.

Federal money would pay to build community mental health centers. It would not pay to run them. Staffing, medication, and ongoing treatment, these costs would fall to states and local communities. It was as if the federal

91

government had agreed to build hospitals but expected someone else to pay for doctors, nurses, and medicine.

Kennedy, had he lived, might have fought for operational funding. He might have used his political capital to ensure the centers were staffed and equipped. He might have monitored implementation, demanded accountability, and adjusted course when problems emerged.

But Kennedy would not live to see his vision implemented.

NOVEMBER 22, 1963: THE VISION DIES

On November 22, 1963—less than one month after signing the Community Mental Health Centers Act—President John F. Kennedy was assassinated in Dallas, Texas.

The man who had championed mental health reform with unusual passion was gone. And with him died any realistic hope that his vision would be fully realized.

Lyndon Johnson, Kennedy's successor, had other priorities. The Vietnam War was escalating, consuming ever-larger portions of the federal budget and presidential attention. Johnson's Great Society programs focused on poverty, education, and civil rights, worthy causes, but ones that left mental health on the margins.

Johnson signed subsequent legislation extending the community mental health program, but without Kennedy's personal commitment, the initiative lost momentum. The promised 1,500 centers were never built. Federal funding remained inadequate. The comprehensive vision of prevention, early intervention, and community integration was never realized.

Instead, what emerged was a patchwork of underfunded clinics that bore little resemblance to Felix's grand design.

The Act called for 1,500 community mental health centers by 1980. By that deadline, fewer than 800 existed, and many of those were centers in name only.

A "community mental health center" might consist of nothing more than a few offices in a strip mall, staffed by one or two therapists with overwhelming caseloads. The comprehensive services Felix had envisioned, emergency care, partial hospitalization, and community consultation, were often absent. There were no beds for patients in crisis. There were no residential programs for those who needed more than outpatient care. There was no structure for people who couldn't manage independently.

By 1990, only 700 centers were operating nationwide, less than half the promised number. Many had closed due to funding cuts. Others had never opened at all.

More fundamentally, the centers that did exist were not serving the people they were designed for.

Felix and Kennedy had envisioned centers that would serve the severely mentally ill—the patients being discharged from state hospitals, the people with schizophrenia and severe bipolar disorder who needed intensive support to survive in the community. But these patients were difficult, demanding, and often unable to keep appointments or follow treatment plans. They required far more resources than the underfunded centers could provide.

Instead, the centers gravitated toward easier cases. They served the "worried well"—people with anxiety, mild depression, and adjustment disorders. These patients were more pleasant to work with, more likely to improve, and more capable of participating in traditional therapy. They made the centers look successful, with good outcomes and satisfied clients.

A 1975 Government Accountability Office study documented the betrayal in stark numbers. Of all patients seen at community mental health centers nationwide, only 23 percent had severe diagnoses—schizophrenia, major depression, and bipolar disorder. The remaining 77 percent had conditions that previous generations had managed without professional help: anxiety about work, stress about relationships, and difficulty adjusting to life changes.

The severely mentally ill, the people Kennedy had spoken about with such passion, the people rotting in "institutional purgatory," were being ignored. The centers that were supposed to catch them when the hospitals emptied were serving someone else entirely.

They were falling through the cracks. Or more accurately, they were falling onto the streets.

THE MOMENTUM BECOMES UNSTOPPABLE

By the time anyone noticed the betrayal, it was too late. Multiple forces had converged to create an unstoppable momentum toward emptying hospitals regardless of whether the promised alternatives existed.

States discovered that they could save enormous sums by discharging patients. The Medicare and Medicaid programs enacted in 1965, two years after Kennedy's death, created perverse incentives that accelerated the emptying.

Neither program would pay for care in state psychiatric hospitals. But both would pay for care in nursing homes, general hospitals, and outpatient settings. States quickly realized they could shift billions in costs to the federal government simply by discharging patients from state hospitals and placing them elsewhere anywhere that would qualify for federal reimbursement.

The cynicism was breathtaking. Patients who had spent decades in state hospitals were discharged to nursing homes that had no psychiatric expertise. They were released to communities that had no services to offer. They were simply turned out onto the streets, where they became someone else's problem or no one's problem at all.

Thorazine and the antipsychotic medications that followed seemed to offer a chemical solution to the need for institutional care. If a pill could control psychotic symptoms, why keep people in expensive hospitals? The medications made administrators and policymakers believe that institutional care was obsolete, that the severely mentally ill could live independently with nothing more than a prescription.

The promise was false or at least wildly overstated but by the time its limitations became clear, the hospitals were already emptying.

One Flew Over the Cuckoo's Nest and similar works had convinced the American public that psychiatric hospitals were irredeemably evil. Any institutionalization was oppression; any commitment was abuse. The possibility that some people genuinely needed long-term structured care became unspeakable in polite company.

A series of court decisions in the 1970s made long-term commitment nearly impossible rulings that, however well-intentioned, had the practical effect of making it illegal to help people who couldn't recognize they needed help. These legal changes will be examined in detail in the next chapter.

Between 1963 and 1980, the population in state psychiatric hospitals dropped from 504,604 to 132,164—a reduction of 74 percent. By 1990, the number had fallen below 100,000. By 2000, it would be below 60,000.

Where did they go? The community centers either did not exist or could not handle them. The nursing homes were not equipped to provide psychiatric care. The families were overwhelmed. The streets were waiting.

Kennedy's beautiful vision, replacing institutional abuse with community care, had created something worse than what it replaced. America had achieved institutional abandonment.

The hospitals emptied. The promised alternatives never materialized. And hundreds of thousands of severely mentally ill Americans were left to fend for themselves in a society that had no place for them.

CHAPTER 5
THE PERFECT STORM

Between 1955 and 1994, America's state psychiatric hospital population dropped from 558,922 to 71,619 a reduction of 87 percent. This wasn't gradual evolution; it was institutional collapse. To understand how it happened, we need to examine the forces that converged to make this transformation inevitable and the consequences that were entirely predictable but somehow went unheeded.

Three rivers fed this flood: legal decisions that made commitment nearly impossible, financial incentives that rewarded discharge regardless of consequences, and an ideological consensus that viewed any institutional care as oppression. Each force alone might have been manageable. Together, they created a catastrophe.

THE LEGAL REVOLUTION: FROM PARENS PATRIAE TO IMMINENT DANGER

For most of American history, the legal standard for psychiatric commitment was "parens patriae," the state as parent. Courts could commit individuals who were mentally ill and unable to care for themselves, on the theory that the state had a duty to protect those who couldn't protect themselves. The standard was paternalistic, easily abused, and often violated civil liberties. But it acknowledged a fundamental reality: some people are too sick to make decisions in their own interest.

The abuses under this system were real and documented. Elizabeth Packard was committed by her husband for disagreeing with him about religion. Immigrants were institutionalized for cultural differences rather than mental illness. Women locked away for "hysteria" or "moral insanity." African Americans were committed at higher rates than whites for the same behaviors. The system needed reform.

But what emerged from the reform movement wasn't a better system. It was the destruction of any meaningful system at all.

The case that changed everything was O'Connor v. Donaldson, decided by the Supreme Court in 1975.

Kenneth Donaldson was committed to Florida State Hospital in 1957 at his father's request. He remained there for fifteen years, despite repeatedly petitioning for release and despite evidence that he could live safely outside the hospital.

The hospital's superintendent, J.B. O'Connor, refused to release him, even though Donaldson had a friend who offered to take responsibility for him and even though he showed no signs of being dangerous.

The Supreme Court ruled unanimously that "a State cannot constitutionally confine a nondangerous individual who is capable of surviving safely in freedom by himself or with the help of willing and responsible family members or friends."

The ruling was narrow; it didn't establish a general right to refuse treatment, and it specifically noted that Donaldson was not dangerous. But its practical effect was revolutionary. States across the country interpreted O'Connor as requiring that commitment be limited to those who were "dangerous," and "dangerous" was increasingly defined as "imminently" dangerous, meaning likely to cause harm in the immediate future.

The shift from "unable to care for oneself" to "imminently dangerous" transformed psychiatric law. Under the old standard, a woman who couldn't feed herself, who was living in filth, who was clearly deteriorating, could be hospitalized for her own protection. Under the new standard, she had a constitutional right to starve on the sidewalk—and the state had no authority to stop her until she actually harmed herself or someone else.

Subsequent cases reinforced and extended this framework.

Lessard v. Schmidt (1972) established that patients facing civil commitment were entitled to the same procedural protections as criminal defendants—lawyers, hearings, and proof beyond a reasonable doubt. The ruling made sense as a matter of due process. Its practical effect was to make commitment proceedings so cumbersome and adversarial that many psychiatrists simply stopped trying.

Addington v. Texas (1979) set the burden of proof for civil commitment at "clear and convincing evidence"—higher than the "preponderance of evidence" standard used in most civil cases, though lower than "beyond a reasonable doubt" required in criminal trials. The intermediate standard was supposed to balance liberty interests against the state's protective role. In practice, it made commitment much harder to achieve.

Rennie v. Klein (1981) and Rogers v. Okin (1982) established that even committed patients had the right to refuse medication except in emergencies. A patient could be hospitalized as a danger to himself, refuse the medication that might restore his sanity, and then be released when the hospital could no longer justify holding someone who wasn't being treated. The circularity was absurd, but it was now constitutional law.

The cumulative effect of these decisions was to create what legal scholar Darold Treffert called "dying with your rights on." The law now protects the right of severely mentally ill people to refuse treatment, live on the streets, eat from garbage cans, and freeze to death in winter, all in the name of liberty and autonomy.

The assumption underlying these rulings was that mental illness didn't really impair decision-making—that a person with schizophrenia refusing treatment was making a choice as valid as anyone else's choice. This assumption contradicted everything clinicians knew about severe mental illness, but it had become legal doctrine.

THE FINANCIAL INCENTIVES: HOW MEDICAID EMPTIED THE HOSPITALS

If the legal revolution made it harder to keep people in hospitals, the financial revolution made it irresistible to discharge them.

The key mechanism was the Medicaid "IMD exclusion," a provision buried in the 1965 legislation that has shaped American mental health policy ever since. IMD stands for "Institution for Mental Diseases." The exclusion prohibits federal Medicaid payments for care provided to most adults in psychiatric facilities with more than sixteen beds.

The policy had its origins in federalism. In 1965, state governments ran and funded psychiatric hospitals. Federal policymakers didn't want Medicaid, a new program with uncertain costs, to become responsible for populations that states had always cared for. So they excluded state psychiatric hospitals from Medicaid coverage.

The unintended consequence was catastrophic.

State governments quickly realized that they could shift billions in costs to the federal government by discharging patients from state hospitals (not covered by Medicaid) to nursing homes, general hospitals, or other settings (covered by Medicaid). The financial incentive to empty state hospitals became overwhelming.

A patient in a state psychiatric hospital costs the state $50,000 or more per year, with no federal contribution. The same patient in a nursing home costs the state perhaps $15,000, with Medicaid covering the rest. The same patient on the street cost the state nothing at all (at least in direct mental health spending; the costs simply shifted to emergency rooms, jails, and homeless services).

The numbers tell the story.

In 1955, state governments spent the equivalent of $42 billion (in 2020 dollars) on state psychiatric hospitals. By 2014, that figure had dropped to $12 billion—a 71 percent reduction. Over the same period, the number of state hospital beds dropped by more than 95 percent.

Where did the money go? Not to the community mental health. State and local spending on community mental health services increased, but nowhere near enough to compensate for the hospital cuts. Much of the "savings" simply disappeared from mental health budgets entirely.

Meanwhile, federal Medicaid spending on nursing home care exploded. By the 1970s, nursing homes had become de facto psychiatric institutions, housing hundreds of thousands of mentally ill elderly people in facilities with no psychiatric expertise, no therapeutic programming, and no intention of providing actual mental health treatment.

A 1977 study found that 25 percent of nursing home residents had significant mental illness. Many had been transferred directly from state psychiatric hospitals. They were receiving no psychiatric care just warehousing in a setting that qualified for federal reimbursement.

The IMD exclusion created a bizarre financial landscape. Federal money would pay for almost any setting except the one specifically designed for psychiatric care. It would pay for emergency rooms but not psychiatric hospitals. It would pay for jails but not treatment facilities. It would pay for homeless shelters but not residential programs.

The policy remains in effect today. Efforts to repeal or modify the IMD exclusion have repeatedly failed, blocked by budget concerns and ideological opposition to institutional care. The result is a mental health system designed around avoiding one specific funding prohibition a system that treats psychiatric hospitals as the one thing Medicaid must never pay for.

THE IDEOLOGICAL CONSENSUS: WHEN EVERYONE AGREED ON SOMETHING WRONG

What made deinstitutionalization possible wasn't just legal and financial pressure. It was an ideological consensus that united left and right, liberals and conservatives, in the conviction that psychiatric hospitals were irredeemably evil and must be eliminated.

From the left came the anti-psychiatry movement, a constellation of academics, activists, and former patients who argued that mental illness itself was a social construct, that psychiatric hospitals were instruments of social control, and that the "mad" were actually prophets and visionaries being persecuted by a conformist society.

R. D. Laing, a Scottish psychiatrist, argued that schizophrenia wasn't a disease but a "sane response to an insane world" that psychotic symptoms were meaningful attempts to cope with impossible family dynamics and social pressures. His books, including The Divided Self (1960) and The Politics of Experience (1967), became counterculture classics.

Thomas Szasz, a Hungarian-American psychiatrist, went further. In The Myth of Mental Illness (1961), he argued that mental illness literally didn't exist that it was a metaphor that had been reified into a false medical category. Psychiatry, in his view, was not medicine but social engineering, using the language of disease to control deviant behavior.

Michel Foucault, the French philosopher, contributed Madness and Civilization (1961), which portrayed the asylum as an instrument of bourgeois social control that emerged in the seventeenth century to confine the poor, the unemployed, and the troublesome. Mental illness, in Foucault's analysis, was whatever society decided to exclude.

These ideas filtered into popular culture through works like Ken Kesey's One Flew Over the Cuckoo's Nest (1962) and its 1975 film adaptation. The novel portrayed psychiatric patients as free spirits crushed by institutional conformity, with the villainous Nurse Ratched representing everything oppressive about medical authority. The film won five Academy Awards and shaped a generation's view of psychiatric hospitals as prisons for the soul.

From the right came fiscal conservatives who saw deinstitutionalization as an opportunity to cut government spending. State psychiatric hospitals were expensive. If patients could be discharged to "community care", which in practice often meant no care at all, states could save billions.

Ronald Reagan, as governor of California (1967–1975), signed the Lanterman-Petris-Short Act in 1967, which made it much harder to commit people involuntarily. He then cut the state mental health budget and closed state hospitals. Similar patterns played out across the country as conservative governors discovered that emptying hospitals was both ideologically satisfying and fiscally advantageous.

The ACLU and other civil liberties organizations provided legal muscle for the movement. They filed lawsuits establishing patients' rights, challenged commitment procedures, and fought to restrict involuntary treatment. Their victories in court accelerated the emptying of hospitals across the country.

What united these disparate groups was a shared conviction that psychiatric hospitals were the problem not a flawed solution to a real problem, but the problem itself. Eliminate the hospitals, and the problem would be solved.

This framing made it impossible to discuss what would actually happen to severely mentally ill people when the hospitals closed. Anyone who raised such questions was accused of defending an indefensible system, of wanting to return to snake pits and straitjackets, of being complicit in oppression.

The result was a policy consensus that brooked no dissent. Democrats and Republicans, liberals and conservatives, activists and bureaucrats all agreed: the hospitals must close. The only question was how fast.

THE REVOLVING DOOR: WHAT REPLACED THE HOSPITALS

As state hospitals emptied, a new pattern emerged that would come to define American mental health care: the revolving door.

A person experiencing a psychiatric crisis arrives at an emergency room. They're evaluated, perhaps admitted to a short-stay psychiatric unit for a few days. Once the acute crisis passes or once their insurance runs out, they're discharged with a prescription and a referral to outpatient care.

The outpatient appointment is weeks away. The prescription requires money and transportation to fill. The person, still symptomatic, stops taking medication within days. They deteriorate. They return to the emergency room. The cycle repeats.

This pattern crisis, brief hospitalization, discharge, deterioration, crisis became the defining feature of mental health care for the severely ill. The average length of stay in psychiatric hospitals dropped from months to days. Readmission rates soared. Patients cycled through the same emergency rooms dozens of times per year.

The numbers are staggering. One study found that 40 percent of patients discharged from psychiatric units were readmitted within thirty days. Another found that 20 percent of all psychiatric hospital admissions were patients who had been discharged within the previous month.

The revolving door wasn't a failure of the system it was the system. Short stays, rapid discharge, minimal follow-up, inevitable relapse. Each rotation through the door generated billing. No one was responsible for long-term outcomes. Success was measured by discharge, not by recovery.

TRANSINSTITUTIONALIZATION: WHERE THEY ACTUALLY WENT

The patients discharged from state hospitals didn't disappear. They were transinstitutionalized, moved from psychiatric hospitals to other institutions that were even less equipped to care for them.

By 2020, more than three million severely mentally ill Americans were in one of three settings:

Jails and prisons. An estimated 383,000 severely mentally ill people are incarcerated in the United States at any given time, more than ten times the number in state psychiatric hospitals. The Los Angeles County Jail, the Cook County Jail in Chicago, and Rikers Island in New York have become the nation's largest de facto psychiatric facilities.

The criminalization of mental illness is now so complete that police officers spend more time responding to mental health calls than to violent crimes. In many cities, calling 911 about a psychiatric emergency will bring police, not paramedics—and the likely outcome is arrest, not treatment.

A 2015 Treatment Advocacy Center study found that there are now 10 times more severely mentally ill people in jails and prisons than in state psychiatric hospitals. The ratio varies by state—in Arizona, it's 30 to 1; in Texas, 20 to 1—but everywhere the pattern is the same: jails have replaced hospitals as the primary response to severe mental illness.

Nursing homes. Hundreds of thousands of mentally ill Americans, particularly the elderly, were transferred from psychiatric hospitals to nursing homes. These facilities had no psychiatric expertise, no therapeutic programming, no intention of providing mental health treatment. Patients were simply warehoused in a setting that qualified for Medicaid reimbursement.

The transfer of psychiatric patients to nursing homes was so extensive that by the 1970s, some observers called it "transinstitutionalization"—the movement of patients from one inadequate institution to another. A 1977 GAO report found that many nursing home residents had simply been dumped from state hospitals with no assessment of whether nursing home care was appropriate.

The streets. This is the most visible and most devastating outcome. An estimated 250,000 to 350,000 severely mentally ill Americans are homeless on any given night. Many cycle between streets, shelters, emergency rooms, and brief jail stays—never receiving consistent treatment, never achieving stability.

These are not people who "fell through the cracks." They are people for whom no cracks exist—because there is no system to fall through. They were discharged from hospitals that were required to release them, referred to community services that didn't exist, prescribed medications they couldn't afford, and left to survive on their own.

THE DEATH OF LONG-TERM CARE

Perhaps the most significant consequence of deinstitutionalization was the near-total elimination of long-term psychiatric care as an option in American medicine.

For some portion of the severely mentally ill—estimates range from 10 to 25 percent—recovery in the traditional sense is not possible. Their illness is chronic, relapsing, and permanently disabling. They will never be able to live independently, hold jobs, or manage their own care. They need long-term structured support, possibly for the rest of their lives.

Before deinstitutionalization, state hospitals provided this care—inadequately, often inhumanely, but they provided it. A person with treatment-resistant schizophrenia had somewhere to go, somewhere that would keep them alive even if it couldn't cure them.

Today, that option barely exists. The total number of state psychiatric hospital beds in the United States is approximately 35,000—down from 339 beds per 100,000 population in 1955 to roughly 11 per 100,000 today. In some states, the number is in single digits.

Private psychiatric hospitals exist, but they're designed for short stays and acute stabilization. Insurance rarely covers more than a few weeks, and costs can exceed $1,000 per day. Long-term private care is available only to the wealthy.

The result is that a diagnosis of severe, treatment-resistant mental illness is now effectively a death sentence carried out in slow motion. Without long-term care options, these patients cycle endlessly through emergency rooms and jails, deteriorating with each rotation, until they die—on average, 25 years earlier than the general population.

We have not eliminated long-term psychiatric care. We have simply moved it to settings streets, jails, emergency rooms, which provide no care at all.

THE PERFECT STORM

The forces described in this chapter, legal, financial, and ideological, did not operate independently. They reinforced each other, creating feedback loops that accelerated the emptying of hospitals far beyond what any single factor could have achieved.

Legal decisions made it harder to commit patients, which reduced hospital populations, which made hospitals seem unnecessary, which encouraged budget cuts, which reduced capacity, which made it even harder to hospitalize people, which provided evidence that hospitals weren't needed, which supported further legal restrictions.

115

Financial incentives encouraged discharge to settings that qualified for Medicaid, which shifted costs from states to the federal government, which reduced pressure on state budgets, which enabled further cuts to state hospitals, which forced more discharges, which increased Medicaid spending on inappropriate settings.

Ideological consensus made it impossible to question whether discharge was appropriate, which prevented course corrections, which allowed the other forces to operate unchecked, which produced visible disasters, which were blamed on inadequate community services rather than on the discharge policy itself.

By the time anyone realized what was happening, the system had already collapsed. The hospitals were closed or closing. The expertise had dispersed. The political will to rebuild had evaporated. The ideological opposition to institutional care had hardened into orthodoxy. We were left with what we have today: an "asylum without walls" where the severely mentally ill wander our streets, fill our jails, and die decades before their time while we congratulate ourselves on having liberated them from the snake pits of the past. The next chapter examines how other nations have approached this same challenge and what they've built that actually works

CHAPTER 6
WHAT OTHER NATIONS HAVE BUILT

Americans often assume that the chaos on our streets is inevitable, that severe mental illness is simply too difficult a problem to solve. But this assumption is contradicted by the experience of other developed nations, which face the same clinical challenges with far better results.

The Netherlands, Germany, Italy, Japan, and other countries have all reformed their mental health systems since the mid-twentieth century. None returned to the old asylum model. But none adopted America's approach of emptying hospitals without building alternatives. Instead, they constructed systems that share a common principle: someone is always responsible for ensuring the severely mentally ill receive care. This chapter examines what these nations built not as models to copy directly, but as proof that alternatives exist.

THE NETHERLANDS: MANDATORY CARE WITHOUT INSTITUTIONS

The Netherlands provides perhaps the clearest example of how a nation can move away from institutional care while maintaining responsibility for the severely mentally ill.

Like the United States, the Netherlands emptied its psychiatric hospitals in the latter twentieth century. Large institutions closed. Patients were discharged to community settings. The rhetoric of "community care" and "patient autonomy" that drove American deinstitutionalization was present in Dutch policy debates as well.

But the Dutch did something America refused to do: they built the community care infrastructure before closing the hospitals, and they maintained legal mechanisms for ensuring that severely ill people received treatment even when they couldn't recognize their need for it. The Dutch system rests on a continuum of care that includes genuine options at every level of need.

At the least restrictive level are outpatient services—psychiatrists, psychologists, social workers, and nurses providing treatment in community settings. These services are covered by mandatory health insurance, eliminating the access barriers that plague American mental health care.

For those who need more support, the Netherlands offers an extensive network of sheltered housing—residential facilities where people with mental illness can live with varying levels of supervision. Some resemble apartment buildings with on-site staff; others provide more intensive support with 24-hour care. Approximately 30,000 Dutch citizens live in such facilities—a rate per capita far higher than anything available in the United States.

For those in crisis, psychiatric hospitals remain available—smaller than the old asylums, but adequate to provide stabilization and intensive treatment. The Dutch have approximately 50 psychiatric beds per 100,000 population, compared to America's 11. This capacity allows hospitals to serve their intended function: treating acute illness rather than serving as warehouses for chronic cases.

Most importantly, the Dutch maintained legal authority to ensure treatment for those who cannot recognize their illness.

The Wet BOPZ (Psychiatric Hospitals Compulsory Admissions Act) governed involuntary treatment from 1994 to 2020, allowing commitment when a patient posed a danger to themselves or others due to mental illness. But "danger" was interpreted more broadly than in American law—it included

119

the danger of serious self-neglect, not just imminent physical harm.

In 2020, the Netherlands enacted an even more comprehensive law: the Wet verplichte geestelijke gezondheidszorg (Compulsory Mental Health Care Act), which allows for mandatory treatment outside hospital settings. Under this law, a person with severe mental illness who refuses treatment can be required to accept it in their own home or in community settings—not just in hospitals.

This is a crucial innovation. American law generally allows involuntary treatment only in hospital settings, which means that the only options are complete liberty or complete institutionalization. The Dutch recognized that this binary choice fails patients who need ongoing treatment but not necessarily hospitalization. Their system allows mandated care in the least restrictive setting appropriate to each case.

The results speak for themselves. The Netherlands has approximately 2,000 homeless people with severe mental illness, in a country of 17 million. The United States, with a population roughly 20 times larger, has 250,000 to 350,000. Adjusted for population, America has roughly 25 times more homeless mentally ill people than the Netherlands.

Dutch prisons hold very few people with severe mental illness—the forensic psychiatric system handles those who commit crimes while mentally ill, providing treatment rather than punishment. America incarcerates 383,000 severely mentally ill people. The contrast could hardly be starker.

The Dutch system isn't perfect. Critics argue that mandatory treatment infringes on autonomy, that community facilities are sometimes inadequate, and that waiting lists for services are too long. These criticisms have merit. But they describe a system that is functioning imperfectly not a system that has collapsed entirely.

GERMANY: COMMUNITY PSYCHIATRY WITH TEETH

Germany's approach shares key features with the Dutch model while reflecting its own legal and cultural traditions.

Like the Netherlands, Germany closed its large psychiatric hospitals in the late twentieth century. The process began with the 1975 Psychiatrie-Enquête, a comprehensive federal report that documented conditions in German psychiatric hospitals and recommended a shift toward community-based care. Over the following decades, hospital beds decreased dramatically while community services expanded.

But Germany, like the Netherlands, maintained legal mechanisms for ensuring treatment. German law allows involuntary commitment not only for those who are immediately dangerous but also for those who pose a significant danger to their health through self-neglect. The standard is broader than America's "imminent danger" requirement, allowing intervention before a crisis becomes a catastrophe.

German states (Länder) maintain responsibility for ensuring adequate psychiatric care within their borders. This federalism could have produced the fragmentation seen in American states, but Germany avoided this outcome through national standards and mandatory coverage requirements.

All German residents are covered by health insurance either through the statutory public system (covering about 90% of the population) or through private insurance. Mental health treatment is covered without the severe restrictions common in American insurance. Psychiatric hospital stays are covered fully, as are outpatient services and medication.

Germany maintains approximately 50 psychiatric beds per 100,000 population, roughly five times the American rate. This capacity allows the system to function as intended:

hospitals handle acute care and treatment-resistant cases, while the majority of patients receive care in community settings.

The Gemeindepsychiatrie (community psychiatry) model provides comprehensive services at the local level. Community psychiatric centers offer outpatient treatment, crisis intervention, social services, and coordination with housing and employment programs. Teams of professionals psychiatrists, nurses, social workers, occupational therapists, work together to support patients in their communities.

For those who need residential support, Germany offers a range of options: therapeutic communities, supervised apartments, group homes, and intensive care facilities. The variety ensures that patients can live in the least restrictive setting appropriate to their condition.

German courts can order outpatient commitment (Betreuung) for individuals who cannot manage their own affairs due to mental illness. A legal guardian (Betreuer) is appointed to make decisions on behalf of the patient, including decisions about treatment. This system provides ongoing oversight without requiring hospitalization. A patient can live in the community while still being legally required to accept treatment.

The results are similar to the Netherlands. Homeless mentally ill people are rare in Germany, estimates suggest fewer than 5,000 nationwide, compared to America's 250,000–350,000. German prisons hold relatively few people with severe mental illness, as the forensic psychiatric system provides treatment rather than incarceration.

Germany's system costs more than America's but it produces dramatically better outcomes. The investment in community services, adequate hospital capacity, and legal oversight pays off in lives saved and suffering prevented.

ITALY: THE BASAGLIA EXPERIMENT AND ITS AFTERMATH

Italy's experience offers both inspiration and caution. In 1978, Italy became the first country in the world to abolish psychiatric hospitals entirely through national legislation, the famous Law 180, also known as the Basaglia Law after the psychiatrist who championed it.

Franco Basaglia was a radical reformer who believed that psychiatric hospitals were inherently dehumanizing. Working at the San Giovanni Hospital in Trieste, he transformed it from a traditional asylum into a therapeutic community, eventually closing it altogether and transferring patients to community services. His success in Trieste inspired national legislation that prohibited new admissions to psychiatric hospitals and required the closure of existing ones.

The Basaglia Law was revolutionary—and its implementation was uneven.

In some regions, particularly in northern Italy, the closure of hospitals was accompanied by the development of comprehensive community services. Trieste itself became a model of community psychiatry, with 24-hour crisis centers, residential facilities, social cooperatives providing employment, and extensive outreach programs. The World Health Organization has recognized Trieste as a model of community mental health care.

But in other regions, particularly in the south, hospitals closed without adequate alternatives being built. Patients were discharged to families who couldn't cope, to communities without services, to streets and shelters. The Italian experience demonstrated both the potential and the peril of deinstitutionalization: it could work magnificently when properly implemented, or it could produce the same abandonment seen in America.

The Italian system today varies dramatically by region. The best Italian programs rival anything in the world. The worst approximate American conditions—though even Italy's worst regions generally have better outcomes than the United States, perhaps because the national health system provides at least some baseline of care.

Italy maintains approximately 10 psychiatric beds per 100,000 population, similar to America's rate. But Italian law requires that these beds be in general hospital psychiatric units, not in separate psychiatric hospitals. Stays are typically short, with community services providing ongoing care.

The Basaglia Law allows for mandatory treatment (Trattamento Sanitario Obbligatorio) under restricted circumstances—when someone is acutely ill, refuses treatment, and cannot be treated outside a hospital. The standard is narrower than in the Netherlands or Germany, but broader than in most American states.

What makes Italy's better regions work is not the absence of hospitals but the presence of comprehensive alternatives. Trieste has 24-hour crisis centers where anyone can walk in and receive immediate help. It has residential facilities for those who need ongoing support. It has social cooperatives—businesses that employ people with mental illness, providing both income and structure. It has outreach teams that actively engage people who might otherwise fall through the cracks.

The lesson of Italy is that community mental health care can work—but only if the community infrastructure actually exists. Law 180 succeeded where it was implemented fully and failed where it was treated as an excuse to cut costs.

JAPAN: A DIFFERENT PATH

Japan presents a contrasting model, one that maintained high levels of institutional care far longer than Western nations, and that is only now moving toward community-based services.

Japan has approximately 269 psychiatric beds per 100,000 population by far the highest rate in the developed world, and roughly 25 times America's rate. The average length of stay in Japanese psychiatric hospitals exceeds 250 days, compared to less than 10 days in most American facilities.

This system has been criticized justly for over-reliance on hospitalization. Many patients remain in Japanese hospitals not because they need hospital-level care but because community alternatives don't exist. The system institutionalizes people who could live more freely with proper support.

But Japan's system, for all its flaws, demonstrates something important: it is possible to maintain responsibility for the severely mentally ill. Japanese cities don't have tent encampments of psychotic homeless people. Japanese prisons don't serve as de facto psychiatric facilities. The mentally ill in Japan may be over-institutionalized, but they are not abandoned.

Japan is now reforming its system, moving toward community-based care while maintaining hospital capacity for those who need it. The 2004 Vision for Reform of Mental Health and Welfare articulated goals of reducing hospital stays and expanding community services. Progress has been slow—institutional inertia is powerful—but the direction is clear.

What Japan's experience suggests is that there are worse things than over-hospitalization. America, in its determination to avoid the problems of institutional care, has produced something far worse: no care at all for hundreds of thousands of severely ill people.

The optimal path lies between Japan's over-reliance on hospitals and America's abandonment. The Netherlands and Germany have found versions of that path. America has yet to look for it.

THE COMMON THREAD: INESCAPABLE RESPONSIBILITY

What unites these diverse systems, Dutch, German, Italian, and Japanese, is a principle that America has uniquely rejected: someone is always responsible for ensuring the severely mentally ill receive care.

In the Netherlands, municipal governments bear legal responsibility for the welfare of residents, including those with mental illness. If someone is deteriorating on the streets, the municipality cannot simply ignore them; there are legal obligations to act.

In Germany, the combination of universal insurance coverage, regional government responsibility, and guardianship laws ensures that someone is always accountable for each patient's care.

In Italy's better regions, comprehensive community services create a web of responsibility crisis centers, residential programs, and employment services that catches people before they fall.

In Japan, the hospital system itself serves as the responsible party, even if the form that responsibility takes is often inappropriate.

129

Only in America can a severely mentally ill person be discharged from a hospital with no plan for follow-up care, no guaranteed access to medication, no housing, no support—and have this be perfectly legal. Only in America can such a person deteriorate on the streets for years while every responsible authority points to someone else. Only in America can that person die on the sidewalk without anyone being held accountable.

This is the core difference. Other nations debate how to fulfill their responsibility to the severely mentally ill— through hospitals or community services, through mandatory treatment or voluntary engagement, through public systems or private providers. America debates whether any responsibility exists at all.

The mentally ill on American streets are not there because we lack resources. America is the richest nation in history. They are not there because we lack knowledge. We know what works. They are there because we have built a system in which their care is no one's job.

WHAT WE COULD LEARN

The international examples in this chapter offer several lessons for American reform.

First, community care requires actual community infrastructure, not just the absence of hospitals. The Dutch sheltered housing system, the German community psychiatric centers, the Italian social cooperatives—these aren't theoretical alternatives to hospitalization. They're real programs with real staff, real budgets, and real capacity to serve people with severe mental illness.

Second, legal authority to ensure treatment is not incompatible with community-based care. The Dutch model of mandatory treatment in community settings shows that the choice isn't between "hospitals with commitment" and "streets with liberty." It's possible to maintain the authority to require treatment while delivering that treatment in the least restrictive setting appropriate to each case.

Third, adequate hospital capacity remains essential even in community-based systems. The Netherlands and Germany maintain 50 psychiatric beds per 100,000 population—five times America's rate. This capacity allows hospitals to function as intended: treating acute illness, stabilizing crises, and providing intensive care for treatment-resistant cases. When hospital capacity is insufficient, the entire system fails.

Fourth, universal insurance coverage for mental health eliminates the access barriers that doom American patients. In every country examined, mental health treatment is covered by mandatory insurance without severe restrictions. No one fails to receive care because they can't afford it or because their insurance refuses to pay.

Fifth, federalism doesn't have to produce fragmentation. Germany is a federal system like the United States, with significant authority residing in state governments. But national standards and coverage requirements prevent the race to the bottom seen in American states.

None of these lessons requires America to adopt any other nation's system wholesale. American culture, legal traditions, and political structures are different, and any reform must account for these differences. But the international evidence demonstrates that better outcomes are possible—that the chaos on American streets is a choice, not an inevitability.

The next chapter turns from international examples to the streets of Los Angeles, where the consequences of American policy choices are visible every day.

CHAPTER 7
WHAT I SEE ON THE STREETS OF LOS ANGELES

I have lived in Los Angeles for more than twenty-five years. In that time, I have watched the city transform into an open-air asylum, an asylum without walls, without treatment, without hope.

Every day, driving through Venice, Hollywood, and downtown, I conduct mental status examinations in my head on people I will never meet. The clinical signs are unmistakable to anyone trained to recognize them. The woman on Spring Street, arguing with invisible tormentors she's experiencing commands auditory hallucinations, voices telling her to do things, voices she cannot ignore no matter how hard she tries. The man on the Venice boardwalk wearing a winter coat in August, layers of clothing piled on despite the heat—he's exhibiting the disorganized behavior characteristic of schizophrenia, his brain unable to process temperature signals properly. The young woman frozen against a building in a posture no healthy person could maintain she's in a catatonic state, her motor system locked by the same illness that has locked her mind.

133

I cannot turn off the clinical eye. I see diagnoses walking down the street, and I know exactly what each person needs and exactly why they're not getting it.

THE NUMBERS

Los Angeles County has the largest homeless population in the United States, approximately 75,000 people on any given night, according to the 2024 point-in-time count. Of these, an estimated 25 to 30 percent, roughly 19,000 to 22,000 people have severe mental illness.

These numbers are almost certainly underestimates. The point-in-time count is conducted on a single night, missing those who cycle between streets and temporary housing. The mental illness estimates rely on self-report and brief screening, missing those too psychotic to participate in surveys or too paranoid to speak honestly with strangers carrying clipboards.

The true number of severely mentally ill homeless people in Los Angeles County is likely closer to 30,000—a population larger than the entire patient census of American state psychiatric hospitals at their peak. But numbers don't capture what I see every day. Let me try to describe it.

SKID ROW: AMERICA'S LARGEST OPEN-AIR ASYLUM

Skid Row occupies approximately fifty blocks in downtown Los Angeles, roughly bounded by Third Street to the north, Seventh Street to the south, Alameda Street to the east, and Main Street to the west. Within these boundaries live an estimated 4,000 to 5,000 people, the highest concentration of homeless individuals in the United States.

Skid Row, Los Angeles (2025)

Skid Row, Los Angeles, is one of the largest concentrations of unsheltered homeless individuals in the United States.

Walking through Skid Row is like walking through the locked ward of a psychiatric hospital—except there are no walls, no staff, no medication, no treatment of any kind. The same symptoms I evaluated in Ohio in 1971 are on display here, fifty years later, but without even the minimal care those institutions provided.

Tents line the sidewalks, some neat and organized, others collapsing into piles of debris. Shopping carts overflow with possessions—the portable households of people with nowhere to store anything. The smell is overwhelming: urine, feces, rotting food, unwashed bodies, and something else, something chemical, the acrid signature of methamphetamine smoke.

And everywhere, the signs of severe mental illness.

A man stands in the middle of the sidewalk, gesturing emphatically, conducting an animated conversation with someone who isn't there. His speech is pressured, rapid, jumping from topic to topic in the "flight of ideas" characteristic of mania. He hasn't slept in days—you can see it in his hollow eyes, his twitching movements. Without intervention, he will crash eventually, perhaps into depression, perhaps into psychosis, perhaps into a confrontation with police that ends in violence.

A woman sits against a building, rocking rhythmically, her lips moving in constant silent speech. She's responding to internal stimuli—the clinical term for the experience of hallucinations. Her eyes track things that aren't there. When passersby come too close, she flinches violently, as if struck. To her, perhaps they did strike her. Her reality is not ours.

A young man lies on the concrete, motionless except for his breathing, in a fetal position he's maintained for hours. This isn't sleep—it's catatonic withdrawal, the body's response to a mind overwhelmed by psychotic terror. In a hospital, he would be evaluated, treated, and gradually brought back to engagement with the world. Here, people step over him like garbage.

These are not unusual sights on Skid Row. They are the ordinary landscape of a neighborhood that has become, by default, America's largest psychiatric facility—except it provides no treatment, no shelter, no food, no protection, nothing except the freedom to die in public.

VENICE BEACH: WHERE TOURISM MEETS TRAGEDY

Venice Beach presents a different face of the crisis—mental illness as spectacle, played out against a backdrop of surf shops and tourists.

The Venice boardwalk stretches for approximately 2.5 miles along the Pacific Ocean, drawing millions of visitors annually. They come for the street performers, the Muscle Beach gym, the medical marijuana dispensaries, the bohemian atmosphere that has defined Venice since the 1960s. What they find, increasingly, is a mental health crisis in plain view.

*Homeless encampment along the Venice Beach boardwalk,
illustrating the collision of tourism, wealth, and untreated mental illness.*

The encampments along the boardwalk have grown
steadily over the past decade. Tents crowd against the
storefronts of upscale boutiques. Shopping carts block the
pathways where tourists once strolled freely. The smell of
marijuana mixes with the smell of sewage from people with no
access to bathrooms.

And among the tents, the severely mentally ill wander
in plain view of beachgoers who avert their eyes and walk
faster.

I watched one morning as a woman, naked from the waist up, walked down the boardwalk screaming at everyone who passed. Her speech was word salad—the fragmented, nonsensical language of severe psychosis, where grammar collapses, and meaning dissolves. "The purple king demands! Electric shadows! They're putting aluminum in my teeth!" Tourists hurried past. Shop owners closed their doors. A police car drove by slowly, its occupants clearly deciding this wasn't worth the paperwork. The woman continued screaming until she exhausted herself and collapsed against a wall, still muttering.

This is Venice Beach in the twenty-first century: million-dollar homes overlooking a population that would have been institutionalized anywhere else in the developed world.

The residents of Venice have organized, protested, and demanded action. Some want the homeless removed by any means necessary. Others advocate for more services, more housing, more compassion. Both sides are frustrated because both sides understand that nothing currently being done is working.

What neither side fully grasps is that the severely mentally ill cannot simply be "housed" into wellness. The woman screaming on the boardwalk doesn't need an apartment, she needs treatment, probably involuntary treatment, probably for an extended period. The current system cannot provide this. So she continues screaming, and the tourists continue averting their eyes, and the residents continue their futile protests.

STREETALIZATION

We have not ended institutionalization. We have merely moved it outdoors. I call this *streetalization*. In the old asylums, patients who remained hospitalized for years underwent a well-documented psychological transformation. They learned the rhythms of institutional life—when meals came, which staff members were kind, how to navigate the social hierarchy of the ward, what behaviors brought privileges, and what brought restrictions. Over time, the institution became their world. The skills required for life outside— managing money, maintaining housing, navigating social relationships, making independent decisions—atrophied from disuse. When deinstitutionalization came, many long-term patients were terrified of discharge. The outside world had become foreign, overwhelming, incomprehensible. The locked ward, however grim, had become home.

I believe the same process is now occurring on our streets.

A person with untreated schizophrenia who has lived in an encampment for months or years undergoes a parallel adaptation. They learn which spots are safest for sleeping, which outreach workers bring food, which other encampment residents can be trusted, how to avoid police sweeps, where to find water, and how to protect their possessions. They develop relationships—however distorted by psychosis—with others in the encampment. They establish territory, routines, and a semblance of predictability in lives otherwise governed by chaos.

The encampment becomes their institution.

And like the institutionalized patients of an earlier era, they come to fear leaving it. The offer of housing—which seems so obviously preferable to those of us with functioning brains—represents not salvation but terror. An apartment means unfamiliar surroundings, loss of the relationships (however tenuous) they have formed, and separation from the only environment they have learned to navigate. For someone whose psychosis already makes the world feel threatening and incomprehensible, the prospect of starting over in a new setting is overwhelming.

This dynamic helps explain the persistent puzzle of service refusal. Outreach teams across Los Angeles report the same pattern: offers of permanent housing refused, sometimes repeatedly, by people living in objectively terrible conditions. The conventional explanation—that these individuals are simply exercising a preference for freedom over rules—misses the psychological reality. What appears to be a choice is often something closer to agoraphobia: a fear of leaving the only environment that has become cognitively manageable.

The parallel to institutional syndrome is precise. Erving Goffman, in his landmark 1961 study *Asylums*, described how total institutions reshape identity, how patients come to define themselves in relation to institutional routines, how the outside world becomes increasingly abstract and frightening. The encampment functions as an informal total institution— unstructured, unsupervised, and brutally dangerous, but psychologically encompassing in the same way. The streetalized person has been shaped by their environment just as surely as the institutionalized patient was shaped by the ward.

This is why 'Housing First' policies, however well-intentioned, so often fail with the severely mentally ill homeless population. We are asking streetalized individuals to abandon their adapted environment without addressing the underlying psychosis that makes any change terrifying. We are asking them to trust strangers, accept help, and relocate to unfamiliar surroundings—precisely the things their illness makes impossible.

The cruelest irony is that the encampment is anything but safe. The very environment to which they have adapted is killing them—through violence, disease, exposure, overdose. They cling to an illusion of security in a place that offers no security at all. Their damaged brains have found a way to make the intolerable feel tolerable, the dangerous feel familiar. And our system, by refusing to intervene, allows this lethal adaptation to continue until it kills them.

Streetalization explains something that baffles observers: why would anyone choose a tent over an apartment, a sidewalk over a bed? The answer is that for someone with untreated psychosis who has spent years adapting to street life, it is not experienced as a choice between bad and good. It is experienced as a choice between the terrifying unknown and the familiar—and the familiar, however objectively terrible, feels safer.

Breaking the cycle of streetalization requires the same thing that breaking institutionalization required: not just offering an alternative environment, but providing the treatment that makes transition possible. Without psychiatric stabilization, without restoration of the capacity to process reality accurately, the streetalized person cannot make use of housing even when it is offered. They need treatment first or simultaneously, not housing alone.

This is what the advocates who oppose involuntary treatment fail to understand. They see refusal of services as an autonomous choice that must be respected. What they are actually seeing is the end stage of a pathological adaptation—a person so deeply streetalized, so thoroughly shaped by years of psychosis and encampment survival, that they can no longer recognize help as help. Respecting that 'choice' is not respecting autonomy. It is abandoning someone to the prison their illness has built around them.

HOLLYWOOD: STARS AND PSYCHOSIS

Hollywood Boulevard, once the glamorous heart of the American film industry, has become another showcase of untreated mental illness.

The famous Walk of Fame—those star-shaped plaques bearing the names of entertainment legends—is now flanked by tents and sleeping bags. Tourists taking photos with the stars share the sidewalk with people in acute psychiatric crisis. The contrast would be absurd if it weren't so tragic: Marilyn Monroe's star, and next to it, a man in the grip of paranoid delusions, convinced that the tourists photographing the sidewalk are actually government agents documenting his movements.

Hollywood attracts the mentally ill for reasons both practical and symbolic. The climate is mild. The tourist economy generates enough cash to support panhandling. The transit system connects Hollywood to services in other parts of the city. And there is something about Hollywood's mythology—the promise of reinvention, of becoming someone new—that draws people who have lost themselves to illness.

I spoke once with a young man on Hollywood Boulevard who told me he had come to Los Angeles to become an actor. He was articulate, intelligent, and clearly educated. He was also clearly psychotic, describing an elaborate plot by rival actors to steal his identity and claim his future fame. His delusions were grandiose but coherent—the systematized paranoia of someone whose illness hadn't yet destroyed his cognitive capacities entirely.

He had been hospitalized twice, he said—once in his home state, once in Los Angeles. Both times, he'd been released after a few days when he stabilized enough to no longer meet the "imminent danger" standard. Both times, he'd stopped taking medication within weeks. Both times, the delusions had returned. Now he was living on the street, convinced that this was temporary, that his breakthrough was coming, that the forces arrayed against him would eventually be defeated.

He was perhaps twenty-five years old. Without sustained treatment, his prognosis is grim: progressive deterioration, repeated hospitalizations, eventual complete disability, and early death. The system that released him twice has no mechanism to ensure he receives ongoing care. He will cycle through emergency rooms and jails until his illness destroys him.

Stories like his are common on Hollywood Boulevard. The aspiring actors and musicians who come to Los Angeles seeking fame, who develop mental illness in their late teens or early twenties (the typical age of onset for schizophrenia), who lose everything to their illness and end up on the streets—they are a significant portion of the homeless mentally ill in this city. Their families, often thousands of miles away, have no power to help them. The system has no power to intervene. They simply deteriorate in public view, their dreams and their minds dissolving together.

THE VIOLENCE

The severely mentally ill are more often victims of violence than perpetrators. This is a statistical fact that advocates rightly emphasize. But it is also true that untreated psychosis sometimes produces violence—and that violence has consequences that ripple far beyond the individual incidents.

Los Angeles has seen a series of high-profile attacks by severely mentally ill homeless individuals. A woman pushed onto the Metro tracks. A nurse was stabbed while walking to work. Random attacks on pedestrians by people in the grip of paranoid delusions. Each incident generates headlines, outrage, calls for action—followed by nothing, because the system has no mechanism to prevent the next attack.

The violence statistics are difficult to pin down precisely, but the trend is clear. Violent incidents involving homeless individuals in Los Angeles have increased dramatically over the past decade. Not all of these incidents involve mental illness—homelessness itself creates conditions that breed violence. But a significant portion involves people who were clearly psychotic at the time of the attack, people whose illness had been known to authorities, people who had cycled through hospitals and jails multiple times before finally committing an act serious enough to result in long-term consequences.

For every violent incident that makes the news, dozens don't. The threats, the harassment, the minor assaults that residents and business owners endure daily. The mother who no longer takes her children to the neighborhood park because a man living there has threatened them repeatedly. The store owner was attacked three times by the same individual — arrested, released, and returned to attack again. The bus drivers who refuse to work certain routes because the danger has become too great.

This violence, both the spectacular incidents and the daily grind of low-level threats, destroys public support for the homeless mentally ill. When people feel unsafe, their compassion evaporates. The political pressure shifts from "help these people" to "remove these people." And since the system can't actually help them, removal becomes the only politically viable option—which means sweeping them from one neighborhood to another, which changes nothing except the location of the problem.

The tragedy is that the violence is preventable. The man who pushed a woman onto Metro tracks had been hospitalized dozens of times. His illness was known. His dangerousness was known. But the system could not hold him, could not treat him, could not prevent him from committing the act that finally resulted in long-term incarceration. If he had been treated years earlier, maintained on medication, and supervised in a community setting, the woman he pushed would still be living, but that would have required a system that doesn't exist.

THE DISEASES

Medieval diseases are returning to Los Angeles. This is not hyperbole. It is a medical fact.

Typhus, spread by fleas that live on rats, appeared in Los Angeles in 2018. The outbreak centered on Skid Row and spread to City Hall, where rats had infested the building. At least one city employee contracted the disease. Public health officials acknowledged that the homeless encampments had created conditions that allowed typhus to flourish for the first time in decades.

Tuberculosis, once nearly eliminated in the United States, persists at elevated rates among the homeless population. The conditions of street life—malnutrition, exposure, crowded shelters, and inability to complete antibiotic courses—create perfect conditions for TB transmission. Drug-resistant strains have emerged, complicating treatment further.

Hepatitis A spread through homeless populations in California beginning in 2017, eventually infecting nearly 700 people and killing at least 21. The outbreak was driven by fecal contamination—people with no access to bathrooms defecating in public, spreading the virus through contact with contaminated surfaces. San Diego responded by pressure-washing the streets with bleach. Los Angeles has not done the same consistently, and the risk of future outbreaks remains.

Skin infections, respiratory illnesses, and sexually transmitted diseases—all are endemic in the homeless population at rates far exceeding the general public. The lack of hygiene, medical care, and nutrition, combined with the constant stress of survival, creates conditions that would have been recognizable in medieval Europe.

And for the severely mentally ill, the situation is worse still. Psychosis impairs judgment about self-care. A person hearing voices may not notice the infected wound on their leg. A person lost in delusions may not recognize the symptoms of tuberculosis. The illness that destroyed their mind also destroys their ability to care for their body.

The average life expectancy for a homeless person in the United States is approximately 48 years, compared to 78 years for the general population.. For homeless people with severe mental illness, the figure is almost certainly lower still. We are watching people die decades before their time, in the richest city in the richest state in the richest nation in history.

THE COST

Los Angeles spends enormous sums on homelessness—and those sums continue to increase while the problem grows worse.

The city and county together spend approximately $1 billion per year on homelessness services. This includes emergency shelters, transitional housing, outreach teams, mental health services, substance abuse treatment, and the administrative bureaucracy that manages it all.
A billion dollars. And the homeless population continues to grow.

The spending on the severely mentally ill homeless is particularly staggering when calculated per person. A 2009 study found that a chronically homeless person with mental illness costs public systems an average of $100,000 per year—through emergency room visits, hospitalizations, jail stays, shelter use, and other crisis services. More recent estimates put the figure closer to $150,000 per year in high-cost cities like Los Angeles.

For that amount, we could provide comprehensive treatment, housing, and support services. We could fund long-term residential care in therapeutic settings. We could pay for supervised housing with on-site psychiatric services. We could do almost anything except what we actually do, which is spend the money on a crisis response that changes nothing.

The spending isn't just wasteful—it's actively harmful. Every dollar spent on emergency room visits for untreated psychosis is a dollar not spent on preventing the psychosis from reaching that point. Every dollar spent on jailing mentally ill people is a dollar not spent on treatment that might keep them out of jail. The system is designed to maximize cost while minimizing benefit.

This is what makes the American approach so inexplicable. We spend more per homeless mentally ill person than any other nation, and we get worse outcomes than any other developed nation. We have proven, conclusively and expensively, that our approach doesn't work. And we continue doing it anyway.

WHAT I SEE

Every day in Los Angeles, I see patients who need treatment and aren't getting it. I see symptoms I recognize from decades of clinical practice, playing out on sidewalks instead of in treatment settings. I see human beings dying by inches, their minds destroyed by illness, their bodies destroyed by the conditions that untreated illness creates.

I see the same thing I saw in Ohio in 1971—severe mental illness in all its devastating forms. The only difference is the setting. In Ohio, the patients were behind locked doors, in a building designed (however badly) for their care. In Los Angeles, they're in plain view, with no doors, no building, no care at all.

We replaced the asylum with the street. We called it progress. And the patients are dying faster than ever.

What I see every day in Los Angeles is proof that our current approach has failed. Not partially failed, not failed to achieve optimal outcomes failed completely, catastrophically, and obviously. The evidence is visible on every major street in this city.

The question is what we're going to do about it.

The next chapter examines the neuroscience of severe mental illness what happens in the brain when psychosis takes hold, and why this knowledge matters for policy. Understanding the biology of mental illness transforms the moral argument for intervention. When we can see that the capacity for decision-making has been destroyed by disease, the case for respecting "autonomous choices" collapses. And with it collapses the legal framework that has made our current catastrophe possible.

CHAPTER 8
THE NEUROSCIENCE OF SEVERE
MENTAL ILLNESS

For most of human history, debates about mental illness were conducted in the dark. We could observe symptoms, describe behaviors, and speculate about causes, but we couldn't see what was actually happening in the brain. Mental illness remained mysterious, its biological basis a matter of theory rather than observation.

That era is over.

Modern neuroscience has given us tools to visualize the living brain in extraordinary detail. We can watch neural activity in real time. We can measure the size and shape of brain structures. We can track the flow of neurotransmitters through synaptic pathways. We can identify which regions activate during specific cognitive tasks and which fail to activate in mental illness.

What these tools reveal transforms the moral and political arguments around severe mental illness. We are no longer speculating about whether someone "really" can't control their behavior or "really" doesn't understand their illness. We can see the damaged brain regions that make control impossible and insight absent. The biological reality of severe mental illness is now visible, measurable, and undeniable.

This chapter examines what neuroscience has revealed about the three conditions most relevant to the crisis on our streets: schizophrenia, severe bipolar disorder, and anosognosia (the inability to recognize one's own illness). Understanding the biology doesn't just satisfy scientific curiosity; it fundamentally changes what we should do about it.

THE SCHIZOPHRENIC BRAIN

Schizophrenia affects approximately 1 percent of the population worldwide, a remarkably consistent rate across cultures, climates, and historical periods. This consistency itself suggests a biological basis: if schizophrenia were primarily caused by social factors, we would expect its prevalence to vary with social conditions. It doesn't.

The symptoms of schizophrenia are divided into three categories: positive symptoms (additions to normal experience), negative symptoms (subtractions from normal experience), and cognitive symptoms (impairments in thinking).

Positive symptoms include hallucinations—most commonly auditory, the "voices" that patients hear—and delusions, which are fixed false beliefs impervious to contradictory evidence. A patient might believe that the CIA is monitoring their thoughts, that their neighbors are poisoning their food, that they have a special relationship with a celebrity, or that they are receiving messages through the television. These beliefs are not simply mistakes; they are experienced with absolute certainty, as real as any other perception.

Negative symptoms include blunted affect (reduced emotional expression), avolition (reduced motivation and goal-directed behavior), anhedonia (inability to experience pleasure), and poverty of speech. These symptoms are often more disabling than the dramatic positive symptoms, because they destroy the capacity for ordinary life working, maintaining relationships, caring for oneself.

Cognitive symptoms include impaired attention, working memory deficits, and reduced executive function the ability to plan, organize, and execute complex behaviors. A person with schizophrenia may struggle to follow a conversation, remember instructions, or complete a multi-step task.

What does neuroscience reveal about the brain changes underlying these symptoms?

The most consistent finding is enlarged ventricles the fluid-filled spaces in the center of the brain. In schizophrenia, these spaces are larger than normal, indicating a loss of surrounding brain tissue. This finding has been replicated in hundreds of studies and is visible even in patients who have never been treated with medication, ruling out drug effects as an explanation.

The tissue loss is not uniform. It particularly affects the prefrontal cortex—the region responsible for executive function, planning, and self-monitoring—and the temporal lobes, which process auditory information and are involved in language. Reduced prefrontal volume correlates with negative symptoms and cognitive impairment; temporal lobe abnormalities correlate with auditory hallucinations.

Functional imaging studies show abnormal patterns of brain activity during cognitive tasks. When healthy people perform tasks requiring working memory or attention, their prefrontal cortex "lights up" with increased blood flow and metabolic activity. In schizophrenia, this activation is reduced or absent—a phenomenon called hypo frontality. The prefrontal cortex is physically present but isn't working properly.

At the cellular level, schizophrenia involves abnormalities in dopamine signaling—the neurotransmitter system that modulates motivation, reward, and the assignment of significance to stimuli. The "dopamine hypothesis" suggests that overactive dopamine transmission in certain brain regions produces positive symptoms (explaining why dopamine-blocking drugs reduce hallucinations and delusions) while underactive transmission in other regions produces negative and cognitive symptoms.

More recent research has implicated glutamate, the brain's primary excitatory neurotransmitter, and the connections between neurons (synapses) that glutamate helps regulate. Synaptic pruning—the normal developmental process by which the brain eliminates unnecessary connections—appears to go awry in schizophrenia, removing too many synapses and disrupting neural circuits.

The key point for policy purposes is this: schizophrenia is a brain disease with visible, measurable biological markers. It is not a failure of will, a lifestyle choice, or a response to social stress. The person with schizophrenia who refuses treatment is not making a free choice with a healthy brain—they are responding to the commands of a damaged brain, a brain that literally cannot process reality accurately.

THE BIPOLAR BRAIN

Bipolar disorder, formerly called manic-depressive illness, affects approximately 2.5 percent of the population. It is characterized by episodes of mania (elevated mood, increased energy, decreased need for sleep, grandiosity, impulsive behavior) alternating with episodes of depression (low mood, fatigue, hopelessness, suicidal thoughts).

The manic episodes are particularly relevant to the crisis on our streets. A person in full mania may go days without sleep, spend money recklessly, engage in dangerous sexual behavior, start grandiose projects they cannot complete, and become hostile when others question their judgment. They feel better than they've ever felt invincible, brilliant, capable of anything. Why would they want treatment for feeling this good?

The neuroimaging findings in bipolar disorder overlap partly with schizophrenia but show distinctive patterns as well.

Like schizophrenia, bipolar disorder involves prefrontal cortex abnormalities. The ventrolateral and dorsolateral prefrontal cortex—regions involved in emotional regulation and impulse control—show reduced volume and activity in bipolar patients, particularly during manic episodes. This helps explain the impulsivity and poor judgment characteristic of mania: the brain regions that normally inhibit reckless behavior are not functioning properly.

The amygdala, a structure deep in the brain that processes emotional information, shows increased activity in bipolar disorder—particularly in response to emotional stimuli. This hyperactive amygdala, combined with a hypoactive prefrontal cortex, creates a brain that overreacts emotionally while lacking the regulatory mechanisms to control those reactions.

White matter abnormalities—damage to the insulated "wiring" that connects different brain regions—are common in bipolar disorder. These connection problems may explain why mood regulation fails: the circuits that should integrate emotional responses with rational thought are literally disconnected.

At the neurotransmitter level, bipolar disorder involves dysregulation of multiple systems. Dopamine and norepinephrine are elevated during mania and depleted during depression. Glutamate signaling is abnormal. The hypothalamic-pituitary-adrenal axis, which regulates stress responses, is overactive.

Bipolar disorder is highly heritable—twin studies show concordance rates of 40 to 70 percent for identical twins, compared to 5 to 10 percent for fraternal twins. This strong genetic component underscores the biological basis of the illness: it runs in families, not because of shared environment but because of shared genes that affect brain development and function.

The policy implications parallel those for schizophrenia. A person in the grip of mania is not making free choices with a healthy brain. The grandiosity, the impulsivity, the resistance to treatment—these are symptoms of a brain disorder, not expressions of autonomous will. When we allow manic patients to refuse treatment because they "feel fine," we are deferring to the judgment of a malfunctioning brain.

ANOSOGNOSIA: WHEN THE BRAIN CANNOT SEE ITSELF

Perhaps the most important neurological concept for mental health policy is one that most policymakers have never heard of: anosognosia.

Anosognosia is the clinical term for lack of insight into one's own illness, specifically, the neurologically based inability to recognize that one is sick. It is not denial in the psychological sense; it is not stubbornness or resistance. It is a deficit in self-awareness caused by damage to specific brain regions.

The term was coined by the French neurologist Joseph Babinski in 1914 to describe stroke patients who were paralyzed on one side of their body but insisted they could move normally. When asked to raise their paralyzed arm, they would confabulate—invent explanations for why they weren't moving it. "I don't feel like it." "I moved it earlier." "My arm is just tired." They weren't lying. Their brain damage had destroyed their ability to perceive their own paralysis.

The same phenomenon occurs in severe mental illness. Approximately 50 percent of people with schizophrenia and 40 percent of people with bipolar disorder have moderate to severe anosognosia. They do not believe they are ill. They do not believe they need treatment. They are not in denial—their brain literally cannot generate the awareness of illness that would motivate treatment-seeking.

The neuroanatomy of anosognosia is now well established. It involves damage to the right parietal lobe and the prefrontal cortex—regions responsible for self-monitoring and metacognition (thinking about one's own thoughts). Brain imaging studies show that patients with schizophrenia who have poor insight have significantly reduced volume and activity in these regions compared to patients with good insight.

REGIONS IMFLICATED IN ANOSOGNOSIA
(LACK OF INSIGHT)

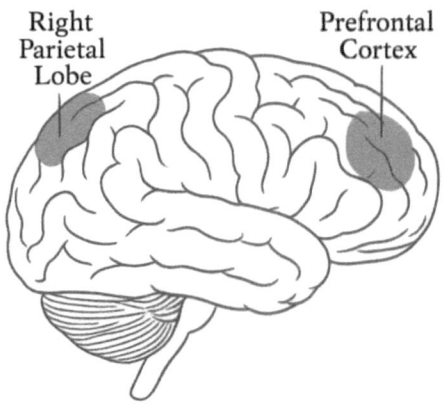

Brain regions implicated in anosognosia (lack of insight), include the prefrontal cortex and right parietal lobe.

The implications for policy are profound.

Our legal system treats refusal of treatment as an autonomous choice deserving respect. If a patient says they don't want medication, we assume they have weighed the costs and benefits and made an informed decision. We may try to persuade them, but ultimately we defer to their stated preference.

Anosognosia destroys the foundation of this assumption. A patient with anosognosia is not weighing costs and benefits—they don't believe there are any costs to refusing treatment, because they don't believe they're sick. Their "choice" to refuse medication is no more informed than a stroke patient's "choice" not to move their paralyzed arm.

This is not a hypothetical problem. Anosognosia is the primary reason severely mentally ill people refuse treatment. Studies consistently show that insight—or its absence—is the strongest predictor of treatment adherence. Patients who recognize they're ill take their medication; patients who don't recognize they're ill don't take it. And since anosognosia is a symptom of the illness itself, the sickest patients are the least likely to accept treatment.

The legal system has largely ignored this reality. Courts continue to treat treatment refusal as a valid exercise of autonomy even when the refusing patient has documented anosognosia—even when imaging studies show the specific brain damage that makes insight impossible. We are allowing brain-damaged patients to make decisions that their brain damage prevents them from making rationally.

This is as absurd as allowing a delirious patient to refuse treatment for the fever causing their delirium. We don't do that—we treat the fever, knowing that the delirium impairs judgment. But we allow psychotic patients to refuse treatment for the psychosis that impairs their judgment, because our legal framework hasn't caught up with our neuroscientific knowledge.

THE PROGRESSIVE NATURE OF UNTREATED PSYCHOSIS

One of the most important neuroscientific findings of the past two decades is that untreated psychosis causes progressive brain damage.

For years, researchers debated whether the brain changes seen in schizophrenia were present from the onset of illness or developed over time. The answer is now clear: both. Some abnormalities are present before the first psychotic episode, but additional damage accumulates with each untreated episode.

Studies tracking patients over time show progressive loss of gray matter the brain tissue containing neural cell bodies in patients with schizophrenia. The rate of loss correlates with the duration of untreated psychosis. Patients who receive treatment quickly after their first episode show less progressive damage than patients whose treatment is delayed.

The mechanism appears to involve excitotoxicity—neural damage caused by excessive glutamate release during psychotic episodes. Psychosis is not just an unpleasant experience; it is actively harming the brain. Every day of untreated psychosis causes additional damage that may be irreversible.

This finding has profound implications for early intervention. The traditional approach to first-episode psychosis was watchful waiting—observe the patient, see if symptoms resolve, avoid the stigma of a schizophrenia diagnosis. Neuroscience suggests this approach is dangerously wrong. Early, aggressive treatment may prevent the progressive brain damage that leads to chronic disability.

It also has implications for the people on our streets. Many have been psychotic for years—decades, in some cases. Each untreated day has caused additional brain damage. Even if they were brought into treatment now, the accumulated harm may be irreversible. The damage we've allowed to occur through our policy of non-intervention is permanent.

This is the hidden cost of our current approach. We tell ourselves that we're respecting autonomy, protecting civil liberties, and avoiding the abuses of the past. Meanwhile, preventable brain damage is accumulating in hundreds of thousands of people whose "liberty" consists of the freedom to deteriorate in public.

WHAT THE BRAIN TELLS US ABOUT POLICY

The neuroscience of severe mental illness is not just academically interesting. It transforms the moral and political arguments about involuntary treatment.

When we can see that a patient's brain is damaged in the specific regions required for insight into illness, the argument that we should respect their "autonomous" treatment refusal collapses. There is no autonomous choice when the mechanism for making autonomous choices has been destroyed by disease.

When we can see that untreated psychosis causes progressive brain damage, the argument that we should "wait until they're ready" for treatment becomes an argument for allowing preventable harm. The patient who isn't ready today will be more brain-damaged tomorrow—and even less capable of being "ready."

When we can see that the same brain regions are involved in psychosis across cultures and centuries, the argument that mental illness is a "social construct" or a "different way of being" collapses. Schizophrenia is not a cultural category; it is a brain disease as real as Parkinson's or Alzheimer's.

None of this means we should return to the abuses of the past. The old asylums were terrible places that violated human dignity in inexcusable ways. But the alternative to bad treatment is not no treatment—it is good treatment. Neuroscience shows us what we're treating and why treatment is necessary. The policy challenge is to provide that treatment in ways that respect human dignity while acknowledging biological reality.

The families of the severely mentally ill understand this. They watch their loved ones deteriorate. They beg for intervention. They are told that their son or daughter has a "right" to refuse treatment—a right that their son or daughter's damaged brain is incapable of exercising rationally. The families know that something is deeply wrong with a system that protects the "right" to die psychotic on a sidewalk.

The neuroscience validates what families have always known: severe mental illness is a brain disease that impairs the very capacities of insight, judgment, and decision-making that our legal system assumes are intact. Until our laws catch up with our science, we will continue to abandon people in the name of respecting their autonomy.

The next chapter examines what families actually experience, the quiet agony of watching a loved one destroyed by illness while a system that could help refuses to act.

CHAPTER 9
THE FAMILIES

The public face of severe mental illness is visible on our streets: the disheveled figures talking to themselves, the tent encampments, the occasional violent incident that makes the evening news. But behind each person on the street is usually a family in quiet agony, watching someone they love destroyed by illness while a system that could help refuses to act.

These families are the hidden casualties of our mental health policy. Their suffering doesn't make headlines. Their struggles unfold in private, in emergency rooms at 3 a.m., in frantic phone calls to crisis lines that can't help, in the slow erosion of hope as they realize that no one not doctors, not police, not courts, has the power to save their child, their sibling, their parent from an illness that is killing them in plain sight.

I have spoken with many of these families over the course of my career. Their stories share common elements: the gradual onset of symptoms, the desperate search for help, the repeated encounters with a system designed to refuse assistance, and the eventual acceptance that they are powerless against both the illness and the legal framework that protects their loved one's "right" to deteriorate.

This chapter tells some of their stories. The names and identifying details have been changed, but the experiences are real, drawn from families I have known, families who have contacted me after learning of my work, and the documented experiences of family advocacy organizations.

MICHAEL'S STORY

Michael was twenty when the illness began. His parents, David and Susan, noticed the changes gradually—withdrawal from friends, declining grades in his junior year of college, strange comments about being watched. They attributed it to stress, to the pressure of pre-med studies, to the normal turbulence of young adulthood.

Then Michael came home for winter break and told them that his professors were part of a conspiracy to steal his research. He hadn't done any research—he was an undergraduate. But he was absolutely certain, and no amount of reasoning could shake his conviction.

David and Susan took Michael to a psychiatrist, who diagnosed "brief psychotic disorder" and prescribed an

173

antipsychotic medication. Michael took the pills for two weeks, improved dramatically, and then stopped taking them. "I'm fine now," he said. "I don't need that stuff messing with my brain."

The delusions returned within a month. This time, Michael believed his parents were part of the conspiracy. He refused to come home, refused to see them, refused to speak to them except to accuse them of trying to poison him. He dropped out of school. He disappeared.

For three years, David and Susan caught glimpses of their son. Occasional phone calls, always hostile, always accusatory. Sightings by friends who saw him on the streets of various cities. A call from a hospital in Denver—Michael had been brought in by police, held for 72 hours, and released. Another call from a jail in Phoenix—arrested for trespassing, released, no charges filed.

"We begged them to hold him," Susan told me. "We explained everything—the diagnosis, the history, the fact that he was clearly getting worse. They said he didn't meet the criteria for involuntary commitment. He wasn't 'imminently dangerous.' He was just homeless and psychotic, and that wasn't enough."

Michael is now thirty-four. He has been hospitalized at least fifteen times, always briefly, always released without follow-up care. He has been arrested at least ten times, always for minor offenses, always released. He has been offered services dozens of times and has refused them all. His illness tells him nothing is wrong; the law protects his right to believe that.

David and Susan don't know where Michael is now. They haven't heard from him in two years. They don't know if he's alive. They have spent hundreds of thousands of dollars on lawyers, private investigators, and treatment programs that Michael walked away from. They have begged every authority they can find for help. No one can help them. No one has the power to help them.

"The worst part," David told me, "is that everyone acts like we're supposed to accept this. Like watching our son die on the street is somehow the right outcome because it respects his 'autonomy.' He's psychotic. He doesn't know he's sick. What autonomy?"

JENNIFER'S STORY

Jennifer was the golden child—valedictorian, soccer captain, accepted to a top university on a full scholarship. Her parents, both teachers, had sacrificed for years to give her every opportunity. She was going to be the first in the family to go to an elite college, the first to have a career that matched her extraordinary abilities.

The first manic episode came during her sophomore year. Her roommate called Jennifer's parents to say that Jennifer hadn't slept in five days, was talking nonstop about a revolutionary theory she had discovered, and had maxed out her credit cards buying equipment for experiments she couldn't explain coherently.

The university health center saw her, diagnosed bipolar disorder, and started medication. Jennifer took it for a month, felt the mania recede, and concluded that she'd been misdiagnosed. She stopped the medication. She didn't tell anyone.

"She seemed fine for almost a year," her mother told me. "We thought maybe it was just a one-time thing, stress-induced. We wanted to believe that."

The second episode was worse. Jennifer dropped out of school mid-semester, convinced that her professors were trying to suppress her discoveries. She drove across the country to confront a scientist she believed was stealing her ideas. She was arrested for trespassing at his laboratory, spent a night in jail, and called her parents from a police station in a state a thousand miles from home.

They brought her back, got her into treatment, and stabilized her on medication. For two years, she was functional not thriving, not the golden child anymore, but managing. She worked part-time, lived at home, and saw a psychiatrist monthly. Her parents dared to hope.

Then she met a man who told her that psychiatry was a scam, that her "gifts" were being suppressed by medication, and that she needed to embrace her true self. She stopped her pills. She moved in with him. She stopped speaking to her parents.

The third episode destroyed what remained. Jennifer had a psychotic break—the mania this time accompanied by delusions, by voices, by a complete break with reality. She was hospitalized, stabilized, and released. Within weeks, she was psychotic again. The cycle repeated: hospital, stabilization, release, deterioration, hospital.

"We tried to get conservatorship," her father said. "Our lawyer told us it was almost impossible in our state. We'd have to prove she was 'gravely disabled'—that she couldn't provide for her basic needs. But she could get food. She could find shelter, even if it was a tent. She was deteriorating, but she wasn't disabled enough for the court."

Jennifer is now living in an encampment in a mid-sized city. Her parents drive three hours every few weeks to bring her food and supplies. She sometimes recognizes them, sometimes doesn't. She refuses to come home, refuses medication, and refuses any help they try to provide. The woman who was going to change the world is slowly dying in a tent, protected by laws that call her refusal a choice.

THE IMPOSSIBLE CHOICES

The families I've spoken with describe a common pattern of impossible choices and decisions where every option leads to harm, where the system forces them to choose between terrible alternatives.

Do you call the police when your loved one is in crisis? Police encounters with mentally ill people sometimes end in tragedy. But what's the alternative? Wait until the crisis escalates further? Try to manage alone a situation you're not equipped to handle?

Do you try to have your loved one involuntarily committed? The process is traumatic, adversarial, and usually unsuccessful. Even if you succeed, they'll be released in days, often angrier and more paranoid than before, convinced that you're the enemy. But what's the alternative? Watch them deteriorate without trying?

Do you let them live at home, even when their illness makes them frightening, even when their delusions target you, even when you fear for your own safety? Keeping them close at least lets you monitor their condition. But at what cost to your other children, your marriage, your own mental health?

Do you cut off contact, for your own survival, accepting that you can't help someone who won't be helped? Some families make this choice, and I don't judge them. But the guilt never goes away. The wondering never stops. Every homeless person on the street could be their child.

One mother told me, "I used to think there were good options and bad options, and if I just worked hard enough, I'd find the good one. Now I know there are only bad options and worse options. And the system isn't designed to help you find even the least bad option. It's designed to make you go away.

THE FINANCIAL DEVASTATION

Severe mental illness doesn't just devastate families emotionally. It devastates them financially.

The direct costs are staggering. Private psychiatric hospitals can cost $1,000 to $2,000 per day. Residential treatment programs run $15,000 to $30,000 per month. Even outpatient care, with psychiatrist visits and medication, can cost hundreds of dollars monthly—more if insurance coverage is limited or denied.

Many families have spent their retirement savings trying to help their loved ones. They've taken out second mortgages, drained college funds, and borrowed from relatives. They've paid for treatment programs that didn't work, for lawyers who couldn't get conservatorship, for private investigators to find loved ones who disappeared.

"We spent $300,000 in four years," one father told me. "Every time we thought we'd found something that might help—a new program, a new medication, a new approach—we tried it. None of it worked because the fundamental problem is that you can't treat someone who doesn't think they're sick and has the legal right to refuse treatment. We might as well have burned the money."

The indirect costs are equally devastating. Parents retire early to care for adult children. Siblings sacrifice their own educations and careers to help manage crises. Spouses are driven apart by the stress, the conflict, and the fundamental disagreement about how to respond to a situation that has no good response.

Studies estimate that families of people with severe mental illness provide an average of 30 hours per week of unpaid caregiving—more than a part-time job, with no training, no support, no respite, and no end in sight. The economic value of this care, if it were paid for professionally, would run into the tens of billions of dollars annually.

Yet families are largely invisible in mental health policy debates. The system treats them as obstacles—people who need to be kept away so that patients can exercise their "autonomy" rather than as resources who know the patient better than any professional, who have been managing crises for years, who desperately want to help if only the system would let them.

THE STIGMA

Beyond the practical burdens, families carry the weight of stigma the unspoken accusation that they somehow caused their loved one's illness.

For decades, psychiatric theory blamed parents especially mothers for schizophrenia. The "schizophrenogenic mother" was a fixture of mid-twentieth-century psychiatry: cold, domineering, unable to provide the emotional warmth that children needed for healthy development. The theory was wrong we now know that schizophrenia is a brain disease with genetic and neurological causes but its legacy persists in the suspicion that families face.

"People look at us like we must have done something," one mother told me. "Like if we'd been better parents, this wouldn't have happened. Nobody says it directly, but you can see it in their eyes. They're wondering what we did wrong."

The stigma extends to social isolation. Families stop talking about their struggles because they're tired of the judgment, the unsolicited advice, the friends who drift away because the situation is "too intense." They withdraw from community activities because their energy is consumed by caregiving. They become invisible, suffering in silence.

Some families describe feeling blamed by the mental health system itself. Privacy laws prevent hospitals from sharing information with families, even when families are the only people trying to help. Doctors refuse to speak with parents because the adult patient hasn't signed a release. The message is clear: you're not part of the treatment team. You're part of the problem.

"My daughter told the hospital that I was abusing her," one mother said. "It wasn't true—it was the paranoia talking. But they believed her. They wouldn't let me visit, wouldn't tell me anything about her treatment, and wouldn't listen when I tried to explain her history. When they released her, they didn't call me. She disappeared. It took me three months to find her."

WHAT FAMILIES WANT

In my conversations with families over the years, I've heard consistent themes about what they want from the mental health system.

They want the legal standard for involuntary treatment to change. The current "imminent danger" standard, they say, means their loved ones must be on the verge of death or violence before intervention is possible. By then, the damage is done. They want a standard that allows intervention earlier when someone is deteriorating, when they're clearly unable to care for themselves, when treatment might actually prevent the worst outcomes.

They want to be included in treatment decisions. Privacy laws, they acknowledge, exist for good reasons. But when a family has been managing crises for years, when they have information that could save their loved one's life, being shut out feels cruel. They want mechanisms that allow families to share information with treatment providers and receive information in return at least in cases where the patient is clearly psychotic, and the family is clearly trying to help.

They want long-term treatment options to exist. The revolving door of brief hospitalizations followed by release to nothing accomplishes nothing except to traumatize everyone involved. They want treatment programs that can hold patients long enough to stabilize them, engage them in therapy, build insight if possible, and transition them to ongoing care with actual follow-up.

They want outpatient commitment to be available and effective. Assisted Outpatient Treatment programs, where they exist, allow courts to order mentally ill people to accept treatment while living in the community. Families generally support these programs because they provide leverage; the patient knows that refusing treatment will result in hospitalization. But the programs are underfunded, underenforced, and unavailable in many jurisdictions.

They want respite. Caring for a severely mentally ill family member is exhausting, and there's no break—no one to take over for a weekend, no vacation from the constant vigilance. They want programs that provide temporary care so that family caregivers can recover before they collapse.

They want, above all, for someone to take responsibility. The current system allows everyone to point at everyone else: hospitals discharge patients because they don't meet commitment criteria; community services don't engage because patients won't accept voluntary treatment; police won't intervene because it's not a crime to be mentally ill; courts defer to "autonomy" even when autonomy is a fiction. No one is accountable when a person dies on the street. Families want a system where someone is responsible for ensuring their loved one doesn't fall through the cracks.

THE NATIONAL ALLIANCE ON MENTAL ILLNESS

The National Alliance on Mental Illness (NAMI), founded in 1979 by a small group of families in Madison, Wisconsin, has become the nation's largest grassroots mental health organization. It represents the collective voice of families who have lived with the system's failures.

NAMI's founding story reflects the experiences described in this chapter. The original founders were parents of adult children with schizophrenia who had discovered, independently, that the system offered them nothing—no information, no support, no treatment that worked. They found each other and realized that their individual struggles were part of a systemic failure that required collective action.

Today, NAMI has over 600 state and local affiliates with hundreds of thousands of members. It provides education, support groups, and advocacy services to families across the country. Its programs include Family-to-Family, a free course that teaches families about mental illness and how to navigate the system, and NAMI Connection, peer-led support groups for adults living with mental illness.

NAMI's policy positions have evolved over the years, reflecting ongoing debates within the mental health community about the proper role of involuntary treatment. The organization has generally supported expanded access to treatment, including Assisted Outpatient Treatment, while emphasizing the importance of recovery-oriented services and peer support.

What NAMI represents, above all, is the refusal of families to accept abandonment as the best available option. In a system designed to make them go away, they have organized, advocated, and persisted. They have turned their private anguish into public activism. They have demanded that someone pay attention to what is happening to their loved ones. The system has not yet listened adequately. But the families have not stopped speaking. The families of the severely mentally ill are not asking for miracles. They know that schizophrenia is not curable, that bipolar disorder requires lifelong management, and that some of their loved ones will never fully recover. They have given up the dreams they once had—the graduations, the weddings, the grandchildren, the ordinary milestones of ordinary lives.

What they ask for is a system that tries. A system that doesn't abandon their loved ones to die on the streets while calling it freedom. A system that recognizes that "autonomy" exercised by a psychotic brain is no autonomy at all. A system that acknowledges their decades of caregiving instead of treating them as obstacles. A system where someone, somewhere, is responsible for ensuring that the severely mentally ill receive care. This is not a radical request. Other nations provide such systems. They cost money, but America has the money. They require changing laws, but laws can be changed. They require political will and that is what has been missing. The next chapter examines what must be built: the legal reforms, the treatment infrastructure, and the systems of care that could replace the asylum without walls with something that actually works.

CHAPTER 10
WHAT MUST BE BUILT

The preceding chapters have documented a catastrophe: America's abandonment of the severely mentally ill to streets, jails, and early death. We have traced the historical arc from Kirkbride's therapeutic vision through the legal and financial forces that emptied the hospitals. We have examined what other nations built and what we see on our own streets. We have explored the neuroscience that reveals why current policies are not just ineffective but biologically absurd. We have listened to families in quiet agony.

Now comes the harder question: What do we do about it?

This chapter proposes a framework for reform not a detailed legislative blueprint, which would vary by state and would quickly become outdated, but a set of principles and structures that any effective system must embody. These proposals draw on international models that work, on the insights of neuroscience, on the experiences of families, and on my own observations across five decades of clinical practice.

The proposals will be controversial. Some will object that they infringe on autonomy, that they risk returning to the abuses of the past, or that they cannot be implemented politically. These objections deserve a response, and I will address them. But first, let me describe what must be built.

PRINCIPLE ONE: INESCAPABLE RESPONSIBILITY

The fundamental flaw in America's mental health system is that no one is responsible for ensuring the severely mentally ill receive care. Hospitals can discharge patients to nowhere. Community services can refuse to engage people who won't accept voluntary treatment. Police can transport people to emergency rooms that release them within hours. Courts can defer to 'autonomy' even when the brain structures required for autonomous decision-making have been destroyed by illness. At every point, responsibility can be escaped.

Any effective system must reverse this. Someone must always be responsible for every severely mentally ill person—responsible not just for offering services but for ensuring that services are actually received, responsible for outcomes rather than just for process.

This principle is not radical. It is how every other serious medical condition is handled. If a patient with diabetes is discharged from a hospital, someone is responsible for ensuring they have access to insulin, that they know how to use

189

it, and that they have follow-up appointments scheduled. If they fail to show up, someone calls. If they're deteriorating, someone intervenes. We don't simply discharge diabetic patients to the street and call it respecting their autonomy when they die of ketoacidosis.

For severe mental illness, responsibility must be assigned and must be inescapable. This likely means a designated agency or entity—what some states call a 'community mental health authority'—that has legal accountability for every severely mentally ill person in its catchment area. Not just accountability for offering services, but accountability for ensuring that people don't fall through the cracks.

Such an entity would maintain a registry of severely mentally ill individuals in its area. It would track their status— hospitalized, in residential care, in outpatient treatment, lost to follow-up. It would have legal authority and practical capacity to engage people who drop out of treatment. It would be held accountable when someone deteriorates to the point of crisis, homelessness, or incarceration.

This is not surveillance for its own sake. It is the infrastructure required to ensure that the severely mentally ill don't disappear into the streets. Without someone tracking outcomes and being held responsible for them, the current pattern will continue: everyone pointing to everyone else while people die on the sidewalk.

PRINCIPLE TWO: A NEW LEGAL STANDARD FOR INTERVENTION

The current legal standard for involuntary treatment 'imminent danger to self or others' must be replaced. But I want to propose something more fundamental than simply lowering the threshold. I want to propose reframing the question entirely.

The problem with 'imminent danger' is not just that it requires waiting for catastrophe. The deeper problem is that it asks the wrong question. It asks: 'Is this person about to cause harm?' The question it should ask is: 'Does this person possess the capacity for genuine autonomous decision-making?'

I propose a new standard: *autonomy-impaired.*

This term directly addresses the foundational premise of current commitment law—that refusal of treatment represents an autonomous choice deserving legal protection. It shifts the legal inquiry from the consequences of illness (danger, disability) to the capacity that illness destroys (the ability to make genuine choices about one's own care).

191

The 'imminent danger' standard made sense as a reaction to the abuses of the past, when people could be committed for being inconvenient, unconventional, or simply female. And 'gravely disabled'—the alternative standard in some jurisdictions—was meant to address those who were deteriorating without being dangerous. But both standards have failed, and for the same reason: they focus on *outcomes* rather than *capacity*. They ask what the person is doing or failing to do, rather than whether the person can genuinely choose.

Gravely disabled' has been gutted by decades of narrow judicial interpretation. Courts have ruled that if someone can obtain food—even from garbage cans—they are not gravely disabled. If they can find shelter—even a tent in a dangerous encampment—they are not gravely disabled. The standard has become almost meaningless, a legal fiction that allows courts to avoid intervening while people slowly die.

Autonomy-impaired' avoids these problems because it asks a different question. It doesn't ask whether someone is *surviving*. It asks whether someone can *choose*. And this question has a scientifically grounded answer.

The neuroscience reviewed in Chapter Eight demonstrates that severe mental illness damages the very brain structures required for autonomous decision-making. The prefrontal cortex—responsible for judgment, planning, and self-awareness—shows reduced volume and activity in schizophrenia and bipolar disorder. The specific regions that enable insight into one's own condition are compromised by anosognosia. We can now visualize these deficits. We can demonstrate, objectively, that the capacity for informed choice has been damaged by illness.

When someone with intact brain function refuses medical treatment, that refusal reflects autonomous choice—even if we think the choice is unwise. But when someone with demonstrable prefrontal damage and anosognosia refuses psychiatric treatment, that refusal is not an autonomous choice. It is a symptom of the illness itself. The brain that is refusing treatment is the same brain that cannot recognize the need for treatment. Calling this 'autonomy' is a category error. It is like calling a delirious patient's attempt to remove their IV an 'informed decision.'

The 'autonomy-impaired' standard would allow intervention based on demonstrated incapacity for genuine choice, not merely on imminent danger or grave disability. This has several crucial advantages.

First, it permits earlier intervention.

Under the 'imminent danger' standard, intervention comes only after crisis—after someone has lost housing, destroyed relationships, accumulated criminal charges, suffered years of untreated psychosis, causing progressive brain damage. By the time someone is 'imminently dangerous,' enormous harm has already occurred. The 'autonomy-impaired' standard allows intervention when the incapacity for choice is demonstrated, before the full cascade of consequences unfolds. Early intervention is both more effective and less coercive—stabilization is easier when deterioration hasn't progressed as far.

Second, it covers the full scope of severe mental illness.

The 'autonomy-impaired' standard captures everyone whose capacity for genuine choice has been destroyed by illness, including:

Those with anosognosia, who literally cannot recognize that they are ill, whose refusal of treatment is itself a symptom of the condition that requires treatment.

Those with severe cognitive impairment, whose psychosis has so fragmented their thinking that they cannot process information about their condition or their options.

Those with psychotic disorganization may understand words but cannot integrate them into coherent decision-making.

Those who have become 'streetatutionalized'—so deeply adapted to life in encampments that they can no longer recognize help as help, who refuse housing not from autonomous preference but from the pathological fear that years of untreated illness and street survival have created.

Third, it is scientifically grounded.

Unlike 'gravely disabled,' which relies on subjective assessments of whether someone can 'provide for basic needs,' the 'autonomy-impaired' standard can be anchored in objective evidence. Neuroimaging can demonstrate prefrontal dysfunction. Standardized assessments can measure insight and decision-making capacity. Clinical evaluation can document the specific deficits that render someone unable to make genuine choices about treatment. This doesn't mean every commitment hearing would require a brain scan—but it means the standard rests on demonstrable biological reality rather than arbitrary judgments about how badly someone must be living before intervention is permitted.

Fourth, it is legally fresh.

Gravely disabled' carries decades of case law that has progressively narrowed its meaning into uselessness. 'Autonomy-impaired' is a new term that courts would interpret without the accumulated weight of restrictive precedent. It offers an opportunity to build a body of law that reflects current neuroscience rather than the legal frameworks of the 1970s.

Fifth, it is philosophically honest.

The current system pretends to respect autonomy while actually abandoning people to their illnesses. It treats the refusal of a psychotic person as equivalent to the refusal of a person with full capacity—a pretense that insults both logic and compassion. The 'autonomy-impaired' standard acknowledges what clinicians and families already know: that severe mental illness can destroy the capacity for autonomous choice, and that respecting the 'choices' of someone who cannot genuinely choose is not respect but abandonment.

How would the 'autonomy-impaired' standard work in practice? A person could be subject to involuntary evaluation and treatment if the following conditions were met:

First, the person has a severe mental illness—typically schizophrenia, schizoaffective disorder, or bipolar disorder with psychotic features. This criterion prevents the standard from being applied to people with milder conditions or to people who are simply unconventional.

Second, the person's illness has demonstrably impaired their capacity for autonomous decision-making about their treatment. This would be established through clinical evaluation, potentially supported by neuroimaging or standardized assessments of insight and capacity. The key question is not whether they are refusing treatment, but whether their refusal reflects genuine autonomous choice or is itself a product of the illness.

Third, without treatment, the person is likely to experience significant harm—not necessarily imminent death, but substantial deterioration in their condition, functioning, physical health, or circumstances. This broader definition of harm acknowledges that people can be destroyed by degrees, not just by single catastrophic events.

Fourth, less restrictive alternatives have been tried or are clearly inappropriate. The 'autonomy-impaired' standard is not a license for immediate involuntary hospitalization. It is a framework for intervention that begins with the least restrictive effective option—perhaps assisted outpatient treatment, or intensive community services—and escalates only when less restrictive approaches have failed.

197

Critics will argue that this standard could be abused—that it could sweep in people who don't need treatment, that it could become a tool for social control. These concerns are legitimate and must be addressed through procedural protections: independent psychiatric evaluations, judicial oversight, time-limited commitments with regular review, robust appeals processes, and clear criteria for what constitutes 'autonomy impairment.'

But the risk of potential abuse must be weighed against the certainty of actual harm under the current standard. The people dying on our streets are not theoretical victims of a hypothetical future abuse. They are real people being destroyed right now by a legal framework that pretends their abandonment is freedom. Every day we fail to act, more people deteriorate beyond the point where treatment can restore them. The 'imminent danger' standard is not protecting these people. It is killing them.

PRINCIPLE THREE: A CONTINUUM OF CARE

An effective mental health system requires a continuum of care a range of treatment settings from least restrictive to most restrictive, with mechanisms for moving people along the continuum as their condition changes.

The current system offers a binary choice: complete liberty or hospitalization. This forces clinicians and courts into impossible decisions. Someone who needs more structure than outpatient care but less than a locked ward has nowhere to go. Someone who has stabilized in the hospital but isn't ready for independent living has nowhere to be discharged to. The gaps in the continuum drive the revolving door of brief hospitalizations followed by rapid deterioration.

A proper continuum would include the following levels:

Outpatient services remain the foundation for psychiatrists, therapists, and case managers providing treatment in community settings. These services must be genuinely accessible, with adequate funding, minimal wait times, and no insurance barriers. For the majority of people with mental illness, outpatient treatment is sufficient.

Assertive Community Treatment (ACT) teams provide intensive, mobile services for people who need more than standard outpatient care. ACT teams—typically including a psychiatrist, nurses, social workers, and peer specialists—go to patients rather than waiting for patients to come to them. They provide medication management, crisis intervention, and practical support (housing, employment, benefits navigation) as an integrated package. Research consistently shows that

ACT reduces hospitalization, homelessness, and incarceration for people with severe mental illness.

Assisted Outpatient Treatment (AOT), sometimes called outpatient commitment, allows courts to order treatment for people who meet specific criteria—typically a history of repeated hospitalizations or dangerous behavior when not in treatment. The patient remains in the community but is legally required to accept treatment. AOT provides leverage that voluntary treatment lacks: the patient knows that failure to comply will result in hospitalization. Studies show that AOT reduces hospitalization, arrest, homelessness, and violence for the population it serves.

Residential treatment facilities provide 24-hour supervised care in unlocked settings. Patients live in group homes or apartment programs with on-site staff who provide medication management, therapy, and daily living support. These facilities are less restrictive than hospitals but more structured than independent living. They are appropriate for people who are stable enough not to require hospitalization but too impaired to live independently.

Crisis stabilization units provide short-term (typically 24 to 72 hours) intensive treatment for people in acute crisis. They serve as an alternative to emergency room visits and brief psychiatric hospitalizations, providing rapid stabilization and connection to ongoing care. Because they're designed specifically for crisis intervention, they can often resolve episodes that would otherwise require hospitalization.

Acute inpatient hospitalization remains necessary for people in psychiatric emergencies—actively suicidal, acutely psychotic, and dangerous to others. Hospitals should provide intensive treatment aimed at rapid stabilization, with clear discharge planning to ensure patients are connected to appropriate ongoing care.

Long-term inpatient care is needed for a subset of severely ill patients who cannot be stabilized through short-term treatment. This is the most controversial element of the continuum, because it resembles the old asylums that reformers worked so hard to close. But the alternative— abandoning treatment-resistant patients to the streets—is worse. Some people need long-term structured care. A humane system provides it.

The key is that all these levels exist, are adequately funded, and are connected to each other. A patient should be able to move from hospital to residential treatment to outpatient care as their condition improves—and back up the continuum if they deteriorate. The transitions should be managed, with warm handoffs between providers rather than the cold discharges to nothing that characterize the current system.

PRINCIPLE FOUR: ADEQUATE CAPACITY

None of the preceding proposals will work without adequate capacity enough beds, enough staff, enough programs to actually serve the population that needs them.

The numbers are stark. The United States currently has approximately 11 psychiatric beds per 100,000 population. The Netherlands and Germany have 50. Even reaching half their level would require quadrupling American capacity.

Achieving adequate capacity requires reversing decades of disinvestment. States must rebuild psychiatric hospital capacity not to recreate the old asylums, but to provide the acute and long-term beds that a functioning system requires. This means capital investment in facilities, ongoing operational funding, and competitive wages to attract and retain staff.

It also requires building the community infrastructure that was promised but never delivered. The community mental health centers that Kennedy envisioned in 1963 were never built in sufficient numbers or funded at adequate levels.

Completing that project sixty years later is essential to any reform.

The cost will be substantial. But we are already spending enormous sums on the consequences of inadequate care emergency room visits, brief hospitalizations, incarceration, homelessness services, and the economic losses from untreated illness. A 2008 study estimated that serious mental illness costs the United States $193 billion annually in lost earnings alone. When we add the costs of healthcare, criminal justice, and social services, the total likely exceeds $300 billion per year.

Much of this spending is wasted consumed by crisis response that changes nothing. Redirecting even a fraction of it toward adequate capacity would improve outcomes while potentially reducing total costs. The question is not whether we can afford to build an adequate system. The question is whether we can afford not to.

PRINCIPLE FIVE: INTEGRATION WITH HOUSING

Mental health treatment cannot succeed if patients have nowhere to live. Housing is not just a social service; it is a medical necessity.

The relationship between mental illness and homelessness is bidirectional. Mental illness causes homelessness when it destroys the capacity to work, maintain relationships, and manage daily life. Homelessness worsens mental illness by creating stress, disrupting treatment, and exposing people to trauma, violence, and substance abuse. Breaking this cycle requires addressing both directions simultaneously.

Housing First is not sufficient by itself. Housing without treatment leaves people isolated in apartments, still symptomatic, still deteriorating, just less visibly than on the street. The most effective programs combine housing with intensive support services: on-site case managers, regular psychiatric visits, help with daily living skills, and social activities that combat isolation.

These programs are expensive, approximately $20,000 to $30,000 per person per year for supportive housing. But they're far less expensive than the alternative. A single psychiatric hospitalization costs more than a year of supportive housing. A year of incarceration costs $40,000 or more. Emergency room visits, shelter stays, social services, and lost productivity add further costs. Studies consistently show that supportive housing for the chronically homeless reduces total public spending, even before considering the humanitarian benefits.

Any serious reform must include a massive expansion of supportive housing permanent housing with services for people who cannot live independently. The current inventory is a small fraction of what's needed. Building adequate capacity requires both funding and overcoming the local opposition that blocks housing development in communities across the country.

PRINCIPLE SIX: INCLUSION OF FAMILIES

Families must be recognized as partners in treatment rather than obstacles to autonomy.

Current policy treats families with suspicion. Privacy laws prevent hospitals from sharing information with families, even when families are desperate to help. Treatment decisions are made without family input, even when families know the patient better than any professional. The message to families is clear: you're not part of the solution.

This approach makes no clinical sense. Families often have decades of experience managing their loved one's illness. They know the early warning signs of relapse. They know what medications have worked and what medications have caused intolerable side effects. They know the stressors that trigger episodes and the interventions that have helped in the past. Excluding this knowledge from treatment decisions is clinical malpractice.

Reform should include mechanisms for involving families in treatment while protecting legitimate privacy interests. At a minimum, families should be able to provide information to treatment providers even if they can't receive information in return. Better yet, patients should be encouraged—and in some cases required—to designate family members who can receive information and participate in treatment planning.

Families also need support in their own right. Caregiver education programs—like NAMI's Family-to-Family course—help families understand mental illness and develop strategies for managing it. Respite services give caregivers temporary relief from the constant demands of caregiving. Family therapy addresses the relationship disruptions that mental illness causes. Support groups connect families who are facing similar challenges. None of these services are adequately available under the current system.

PRINCIPLE SEVEN: ACCOUNTABILITY AND OVERSIGHT

Any system that exercises coercive authority over individuals must be subject to rigorous oversight to prevent abuse.

The abuses of the old asylum system were real. People were committed without due process, held for decades without review, and subjected to treatments that ranged from useless to horrific. Any reform must include safeguards against repeating these abuses.

Judicial oversight is essential. Involuntary commitment should require court approval, with the patient represented by counsel and given the opportunity to contest the commitment. Commitments should be time-limited, with mandatory review hearings at regular intervals. Patients should have the right to appeal adverse decisions.

Independent monitoring is equally important. Psychiatric facilities should be subject to unannounced inspections by independent ombudsmen. Patient rights offices should investigate complaints and have the authority to enforce corrections. Quality metrics should be collected and publicly reported, allowing comparison across facilities and systems.

Transparency requirements ensure accountability. Aggregate data on commitments, lengths of stay, treatment outcomes, and patient complaints should be publicly available. This allows researchers, advocates, and policymakers to identify problems and evaluate reforms.

These safeguards add cost and complexity to the system. They slow down decision-making and create bureaucratic burdens. But they are the price of exercising coercive authority legitimately. A system that can involuntarily commit people must prove that it does so appropriately. The alternative abandoning oversight to preserve 'efficiency' would recreate the conditions that made the old asylums so abusive.

ADDRESSING THE OBJECTIONS

These proposals will face objections from multiple directions. Let me address the most significant ones.

'This infringes on autonomy.' Yes, it does. Involuntary treatment, by definition, overrides individual choice. The question is whether that infringement is justified.

The autonomy objection assumes that the person refusing treatment is making an informed, rational choice that deserves respect. But the entire point of the 'autonomy-impaired' standard is that for many severely mentally ill people, this assumption is demonstrably false. A person with anosognosia cannot understand that they are ill—their brain literally lacks the capacity for that insight. A person with severe prefrontal dysfunction cannot weigh options and consequences in the way that autonomous decision-making requires. Their 'choice' to refuse treatment is not an exercise of rational autonomy; it is a symptom of the illness that has destroyed their capacity for rational autonomy.

To call this 'respecting autonomy' is Orwellian. We are not respecting their autonomy; we are abandoning them to an illness that has stolen their autonomy. True respect for persons requires recognizing when they cannot exercise genuine choice and acting to restore that capacity when possible.

Moreover, autonomy is not the only value at stake. The person left untreated loses more than their health. They lose their relationships, their housing, their future, their very self. The families who watch them deteriorate lose their loved ones. The communities where they live lose safety and livability. A proper balancing of values considers all these harms, not just the infringement on a 'choice' that was never genuinely autonomous to begin with.

'This could return us to the abuses of the past.

This concern is legitimate. The old asylums were terrible places that violated human dignity. Any reform must include safeguards against recreating those conditions.

But the appropriate response to past abuse is not to eliminate the capacity for intervention. It is to exercise that capacity responsibly, with oversight, accountability, and respect for human dignity. We don't abolish prisons because of prison abuse; we reform them. We don't abolish hospitals because of medical malpractice; we regulate them. The same logic applies to psychiatric treatment.

The current system hasn't eliminated abuse. It has simply changed its form. The people dying on our streets are being abused by neglect, by abandonment, by a society that has decided their suffering is acceptable. That this abuse occurs outside institutional walls doesn't make it less abusive. We have traded the abuse of confinement for the abuse of abandonment, and the latter is killing more people.

This is politically impossible.

Perhaps. The interests arrayed against reform are powerful: civil liberties organizations committed to the current legal framework, fiscal conservatives opposed to new spending, NIMBY (Not In My Back Yard) sentiment against building treatment facilities, and a general public that prefers not to think about mental illness at all.

But political impossibility is not permanent. Attitudes change, coalitions shift, crises create opportunities. The homelessness crisis is becoming impossible to ignore. The jails are overflowing with mentally ill people. The families are organizing and demanding change. The status quo is increasingly indefensible.

What's needed is a clear vision of what should replace it. That's what this chapter has tried to provide—not a detailed political strategy, but a framework for what an effective system would look like. When the political moment arrives, reformers need to know what they're building.

THE COST OF INACTION

The proposals in this chapter would cost money billions of dollars annually, at scale. This is the final objection, and it deserves a direct answer.

Yes, building an adequate mental health system is expensive. So is the current system of failure. We spend billions on emergency rooms, jails, homeless services, and crisis response. We lose billions more in productivity, in destroyed families, in communities degraded by visible suffering. We pay the cost of severe mental illness one way or another. The only question is whether we pay it in a way that helps people or in a way that abandons them.

The people dying on our streets are not saved by our refusal to spend money on their care. They simply die cheaper—or rather, they die while we spend the money elsewhere, on responses that change nothing.

The richest nation in history can afford to care for its most vulnerable citizens. The question is whether we choose to.

The next chapter turns from policy proposals to the deeper question of why this matters—the moral argument for treating the severely mentally ill as human beings deserving of care rather than autonomous agents deserving of neglect.

CHAPTER 11
THE MORAL ARGUMENT

T he previous chapter laid out what must be built the infrastructure, the legal standards, the systems of care that could replace the asylum without walls. But policy proposals, however sound, cannot succeed without moral clarity about why they matter. This chapter addresses the deeper question: What do we owe to those whose minds have failed them?

The debate over mental health policy is, at its core, a debate about competing moral values. On one side stands autonomy the principle that individuals have the right to make their own choices, including bad choices, without interference from others. On the other side stands beneficence the obligation to help those who cannot help themselves, even when they don't want help. American policy has elevated autonomy to near-absolute status, treating any involuntary intervention as a violation of fundamental rights. This chapter argues that this elevation is morally mistaken that a proper understanding of both autonomy and human dignity requires a different balance.

THE AUTONOMY ILLUSION

The moral case for the current system rests on the principle of autonomy: every person has the right to make their own decisions about their life, including decisions about medical treatment. If someone with schizophrenia chooses to refuse medication, live on the street, and eat from garbage cans, that is their right. We may offer help, but we may not impose it. To do otherwise would be paternalism—the arrogant assumption that we know better than they do what is good for them.

This argument has a powerful intuitive appeal. We rightly recoil from a society where the state can override individual choices simply because it disapproves of them. We remember the abuses of the past—women committed for "hysteria," dissidents labeled insane, minorities institutionalized for being different. The autonomy principle protects against these abuses by requiring that we respect individual choices even when we disagree with them.

But the autonomy argument contains a fatal assumption: that the person refusing treatment is capable of making an autonomous choice. For many severely mentally ill people, this assumption is false.

Autonomy, properly understood, requires certain cognitive capacities. An autonomous choice is one made by a person who understands the relevant information, can reason about the consequences of different options, and can act in accordance with their own values and goals. This is what distinguishes an autonomous choice from a reflex, an impulse, or a delusion.

Severe mental illness destroys these capacities. A person with anosognosia cannot understand the relevant information specifically, the information that they are ill. A person in the grip of paranoid delusions cannot reason about consequences their reasoning is distorted by false premises. A person whose illness has disconnected them from their own values and goals cannot act in accordance with them.

When we "respect" the treatment refusal of someone with severe anosognosia, we are not respecting an autonomous choice. We are deferring to a symptom. The person is not choosing to refuse treatment in any meaningful sense; their damaged brain is generating a refusal that the person, if they could step outside their illness, might not endorse.

Consider an analogy. A patient with severe Alzheimer's disease refuses to eat. They don't recognize food as food; they don't remember that eating is necessary for survival; they don't understand that refusing to eat will kill them. Do we "respect their autonomy" by letting them starve? Of course not. We recognize that the dementia has destroyed the capacities required for autonomous choice, and we provide nutrition even over their objection.

The same logic applies to severe psychosis. When anosognosia prevents someone from recognizing their illness, they cannot make an informed decision about treatment. When delusions distort their reasoning, they cannot weigh costs and benefits rationally. When negative symptoms destroy motivation and initiative, they cannot act on whatever preferences they might have. The "choice" to refuse treatment is not autonomous; it is a manifestation of the illness that treatment would address.

This doesn't mean that all mentally ill people lack autonomy. Many people with mental illness retain full decision-making capacity and should have their choices respected absolutely. The argument applies specifically to those whose illness has destroyed the capacities that autonomy requires and neuroscience now allows us to identify these cases with increasing precision.

WHAT DIGNITY REQUIRES

If autonomy doesn't settle the question, what does? I suggest that the relevant value is dignity and that dignity, properly understood, supports intervention rather than abandonment.

Dignity is a contested concept, but at its core it refers to the inherent worth of human beings the value that every person possesses simply by virtue of being human, regardless of their circumstances, capacities, or choices. Dignity is not earned or lost; it is not contingent on what one does or becomes. It is the foundation of human rights, the basis for the moral claim that every person deserves to be treated as an end in themselves, never merely as a means.

What does dignity require in the context of severe mental illness?

One answer the answer implicit in current policy—is that dignity requires respecting choices. A person's dignity is honored when we let them live as they choose, even if we disagree with their choices. Intervention is an affront to dignity because it treats the person as incapable of directing their own life.

But this answer makes dignity entirely dependent on autonomy. If someone lacks the capacity for autonomous choice as many severely mentally ill people do—then dignity, on this view, has no application. The person without decision-making capacity has no claim to anything; they can be ignored, abandoned, left to rot, and dignity is not violated because there's no autonomy to respect.

This cannot be right. Dignity is supposed to be inherent possessed by all humans regardless of their capacities. If dignity requires autonomy, then infants have no dignity, people with severe dementia have no dignity, people in comas have no dignity. We don't believe this. We believe that these individuals retain their dignity and that their dignity makes claims on us claims to care, to protection, to treatment of their interests as mattering.

A better understanding of dignity recognizes that it has multiple dimensions. One dimension is indeed autonomy the dignity of being able to direct one's own life. But another dimension is welfare the dignity of having one's basic needs met, of being free from unnecessary suffering, of being treated as a being whose well-being matters. And another dimension is social recognition the dignity of being seen, acknowledged, included in the moral community rather than cast out of it.

When we leave a psychotic person to deteriorate on the street, we may be "respecting" their autonomy (though, as argued above, this is illusory). But we are violating their dignity in every other dimension. We are not meeting their basic needs. We are allowing unnecessary suffering. We are treating them as beings whose well-being doesn't matter. We are excluding them from the moral community, making them invisible, denying them the social recognition that affirms their humanity.

The person dying on the sidewalk covered in filth, eating garbage, talking to hallucinations, ignored by passersby is not living a dignified life. Their "freedom" is not dignity; it is abandonment dressed up in the language of rights. A society that permits this is not honoring human dignity. It is betraying it.

THE ETHICS OF RESCUE

Consider a different moral framework: the ethics of rescue. We generally believe that when someone is in serious danger and we can help them at reasonable cost to ourselves, we have an obligation to do so. If you see a child drowning in a shallow pond and you can save them by wading in, you should do it. The obligation holds even if the rescue is unwanted—we don't ask the drowning child for consent before pulling them out.

The severely mentally ill person on the street is drowning—slowly, in public, over months or years rather than minutes. They are in serious danger: of illness, of violence, of exposure, of early death. We can help them, at reasonable cost—the interventions described in the previous chapter are expensive but not impossibly so, especially compared to what we already spend on ineffective crisis response.

The ethics of rescue suggests that we have an obligation to help. This obligation is not negated by the person's refusal, because the refusal is itself a symptom of the drowning. We don't let the delirious swimmer reject rescue because they believe they can fly. We don't let the hypothermic hiker refuse warming because their confusion makes them feel hot. We recognize that certain conditions impair judgment about the very help that would restore it—and we help anyway, knowing that the person, once rescued, will likely be grateful.

The mental health data supports this expectation. Studies of patients who were involuntarily committed and successfully treated consistently show that a majority, in retrospect, are grateful for the intervention. They recognize that their illness prevented them from accepting help voluntarily, and they appreciate that someone intervened despite their objections. The anticipated gratitude of the rescued self—the self that will exist after successful treatment—provides moral warrant for overriding the objections of the ill self.

This is not a blanket justification for paternalism. The ethics of rescue applies only when the danger is serious, the rescue is likely to succeed, and the person's refusal is plausibly attributable to the condition that makes rescue necessary. It doesn't justify intervention for minor illnesses, uncertain treatments, or competent refusals. But for the severely mentally ill person whose illness prevents them from recognizing their need for treatment, it provides strong moral grounds for intervention.

THE FAILURE OF NEGATIVE LIBERTY

Philosophers distinguish between negative liberty (freedom from interference) and positive liberty (freedom to live a flourishing life). The current mental health system maximizes negative liberty: it protects the severely mentally ill from the interference of treatment. But it does nothing to promote positive libertythe actual capacity to live a meaningful, fulfilling life.

A person with untreated schizophrenia has abundant negative liberty. No one forces them to take medication. No one confines them in hospitals. No one interferes with their choices. They are free—free to live in filth, free to eat from garbage, free to die decades before their time.

221

But they have no positive liberty. They cannot pursue their goals because their illness has destroyed their capacity to form and pursue goals. They cannot maintain relationships because their symptoms drive others away. They cannot work because they cannot function. They cannot participate in civic life because they are excluded from the community. Their "freedom" from interference coexists with complete unfreedom in any substantive sense.

What good is the freedom to refuse treatment if the result is the destruction of everything that makes life worth living? The person who exercises this freedom ends up with nothing—no relationships, no work, no home, no future, no self. They have maximized negative liberty at the cost of annihilating positive liberty.

A morally adequate policy would aim at positive liberty—at restoring the capacity to live a meaningful life. This may require temporary constraints on negative liberty: involuntary treatment, supervised housing, and mandated medication. But these constraints are in service of a greater freedom—the freedom to be oneself again, to pursue one's goals, to participate in community, to live rather than merely exist.

The opponents of involuntary treatment focus entirely on what is lost—the freedom from interference. They ignore what is gained—the freedom to live. A proper moral accounting considers both sides of the ledger. When the gain in positive liberty outweighs the loss in negative liberty—when treatment can restore someone to a meaningful life—intervention is not just permitted but required.

THE CLAIMS OF COMMUNITY

So far, the argument has focused on what we owe to the severely mentally ill themselves. But there are other stakeholders whose claims deserve consideration: families, neighbors, and communities.

Families bear the heaviest burden of untreated mental illness. They watch their loved ones deteriorate. They endure the fear, the disruption, the financial devastation. They are expected to manage crises they're not equipped to handle and to accept outcomes they never chose. The autonomy of the mentally ill person is protected; the autonomy of the family, their right to peace, to safety, to a life not dominated by someone else's illness, is ignored.

When we refuse to treat a severely mentally ill person against their will, we are not avoiding coercion. We are shifting the burden of the illness onto people who have no say in the matter. The family didn't choose to have a mentally ill relative. They didn't consent to years of caregiving. Their lives are constrained, their choices narrowed, their freedom compromised—all in the name of respecting the "autonomy" of someone whose autonomy is illusory.

Communities, too, bear costs. The homeless encampments that have spread across American cities with their crime, their disorder, their public health hazards, are not victimless. They degrade neighborhoods, drive away businesses, make public spaces unusable, and create fear that constrains the freedom of everyone who lives nearby. These harms fall disproportionately on the poor and vulnerable, who cannot afford to move to neighborhoods where the mentally ill are someone else's problem.

The claims of family and community do not override the interests of the mentally ill person. But they are part of the moral equation. A policy that maximizes one person's negative liberty while imposing serious harms on everyone around them is not obviously just. A proper moral framework considers all affected parties and seeks a balance that acknowledges everyone's legitimate interests.

THE LESSONS OF NEUROSCIENCE REVISITED

The neuroscience discussed in Chapter 8 is not just scientifically interesting; it is morally transformative. When we can see that psychosis involves structural brain abnormalities, that anosognosia results from damage to specific neural circuits, that untreated illness causes progressive brain damage, the moral landscape shifts.

The autonomy argument depends on the premise that the person refusing treatment has the capacity for informed choice. Neuroscience shows that this premise is often false. We can now identify the brain damage that makes insight impossible. We can visualize the neural dysfunction that distorts reasoning. We can measure the progressive deterioration that untreated illness causes.

This knowledge obligates us to act differently. We can no longer tell ourselves that we're respecting autonomy when we defer to a psychotic patient's refusal. We know not just suspect, but know that their brain is damaged in the specific regions required for the decisions we're asking them to make. We know that their "choice" is being generated by a malfunctioning organ, not by a reasoning mind.

Neuroscience also reveals the stakes. Every day of untreated psychosis causes additional brain damage. The

225

person we're "respecting" today will be more impaired tomorrow, less capable of recovery, further from the self they would be if treated. Our restraint is not neutral; it is actively harmful. We are allowing preventable brain damage in the name of a principle that doesn't apply.

When morality and neuroscience converge this clearly, action is required. We cannot claim ignorance. We cannot hide behind abstractions about autonomy when we can see the damaged brain on the scan. We are making a choice to treat or to abandon, and we must own the consequences of that choice.

A DIFFERENT VISION

Imagine a different approach—one that takes dignity seriously in all its dimensions, that rescues the drowning rather than respecting their refusal, that aims at positive liberty rather than mere negative liberty, that acknowledges the claims of family and community, that acts on what neuroscience reveals.

In this vision, we would intervene early, before years of deterioration, before progressive brain damage, before homelessness and incarceration. We would provide treatment not as punishment but as rescue, with the same urgency we would bring to any medical emergency. We would maintain oversight and accountability to prevent abuse, but we would not allow the fear of abuse to paralyze us into inaction.

We would aim at restoration rather than mere stabilization. The goal would not be to make the person less troublesome but to help them become themselves again to recover the capacities that illness has stolen, to reconnect with the goals and values they held before psychosis reshaped their brain. Treatment would be in service of the person's own deepest interests, not imposed alien values.

We would include families as partners, recognizing their knowledge, their commitment, and their suffering. We would provide them with support, respite, and resources rather than treating them as obstacles. We would acknowledge that healing happens in a relationship, not in isolation.

We would build the infrastructure required to make this vision real the treatment facilities, the housing, the community services, the continuum of care. We would fund it adequately, recognizing that the investment saves money in the long run and saves lives immediately.

This vision is not utopian. Elements of it exist in other countries and in scattered programs across America. It is achievable if we choose to achieve it. The barriers are not technical or financial. They are moral and political convictions that the current approach is acceptable, that the suffering on

227

our streets is the price of freedom, that nothing better is possible.

This chapter has argued that the current approach is not acceptable that it rests on a misunderstanding of autonomy, a truncated conception of dignity, and a willful blindness to what neuroscience reveals. The suffering on our streets is not the price of freedom; it is the consequence of abandonment. Something better is not just possible but morally required.

The final chapter looks forward at what it would take to build the system we need, at the signs of change already emerging, and at the hope that, perhaps, we might finally get this right.

CHAPTER 12
CONCLUSION

I began this book with a walk through the locked wards of an Ohio state hospital in 1971, where I saw the end stage of the old asylum system overcrowded, underfunded, warehousing human beings who had been forgotten by the world. I have spent the intervening pages tracing how we arrived at something worse: an asylum without walls, where the severely mentally ill wander our streets, fill our jails, and die decades before their time.

The journey has taken us through five thousand years of human struggle with madness—from the bimaristans of medieval Baghdad to the Kirkbride asylums of nineteenth-century America, from the legal revolution that emptied our hospitals to the neuroscience that reveals why our current approach is biologically absurd. We have listened to families in quiet agony and examined what other nations have built. We have confronted the moral questions that policy debates so often avoid.

Now, in this final chapter, I want to step back and ask: Is there reason for hope? Can we actually build something better? And what might that building require of us?

WHAT WE HAVE LEARNED

Let me summarize what I believe this book has established.

First, severe mental illness is real a biological condition that affects roughly 1 to 2 percent of the population across all cultures and all times. It is not a social construct, not a different way of being, not a response to capitalism or family dysfunction. It is a brain disease, as real as cancer or heart disease, and it requires medical treatment.

Second, some portion of the severely mentally ill cannot recognize their illness or accept treatment voluntarily. Anosognosia the neurologically based inability to perceive one's own condition affects approximately half of those with schizophrenia and 40 percent of those with bipolar disorder. For these individuals, voluntary treatment is not an option. They will refuse help until they die, not because they are stubborn but because their brain damage makes insight impossible.

Third, untreated severe mental illness is progressive and often fatal. Every episode of psychosis causes additional brain damage. The person who is merely symptomatic today will be more impaired tomorrow. Left untreated, severe mental illness leads to homelessness, incarceration, and early death on average, 25 years earlier than the general population.

Fourth, the current American approach maximizing negative liberty while providing minimal care has failed catastrophically. We have achieved the worst of all worlds: the highest costs and the worst outcomes in the developed world. We spend more per homeless mentally ill person than any other nation and get less for it. The system is not just suboptimal; it is actively destructive.

Fifth, other nations have done better. The Netherlands, Germany, and other developed democracies have built systems that provide comprehensive care while maintaining legal protections against abuse. These systems are not perfect, but they prove that alternatives exist. American exceptionalism in this domain is not something to be proud of.

Sixth, the moral framework that justifies our current approach is incoherent. It rests on a conception of autonomy that doesn't apply to people whose illness has destroyed their capacity for autonomous choice. It privileges negative liberty while ignoring positive liberty. It treats abandonment as respect and allows people to die in the name of freedom. This framework must be replaced with one that takes human dignity seriously in all its dimensions.

THE SIGNS OF CHANGE

Is there reason to believe that change is coming?

The honest answer is: perhaps. The political landscape is not entirely bleak. There are signs that the consensus that produced our current catastrophe may be fracturing.

The homelessness crisis has become impossible to ignore. Cities across America are confronting encampments, public disorder, and visible suffering on a scale not seen in generations. The issue has moved from specialized policy debates to front-page news, from academic conferences to neighborhood meetings. Politicians who once avoided the topic now find that voters demand action.

The pendulum of public opinion may be swinging. Polls consistently show that Americans support more mental health treatment, including involuntary treatment for those who cannot recognize their illness. The ideological consensus that opposed any coercive intervention—the coalition of civil libertarians, fiscal conservatives, and anti-psychiatry activists is losing its grip. People are seeing the consequences of that consensus on their streets, and they don't like what they see.

Some states are expanding Assisted Outpatient Treatment programs and making them easier to use.

California's CARE Court, enacted in 2022, creates a new civil court process to connect people with severe mental illness to treatment and support services before they cycle through emergency rooms and jails. The program is imperfect and underfunded, but it represents a significant shift in a state that has long resisted involuntary intervention.

The Treatment Advocacy Center, NAMI, and other organizations continue to advocate for reform. Families who once suffered in silence are organizing, speaking out, and demanding that lawmakers confront what their policies have produced. The moral authority of those who have lived with the system's failures is increasingly difficult to dismiss.

Neuroscience is providing new arguments and new tools. Brain imaging studies that document anosognosia, progressive brain damage from untreated psychosis, and the biological basis of severe mental illness are entering legal and policy debates. The claim that we should respect the "autonomy" of someone whose brain damage is visible on a scan is becoming harder to sustain.

None of this guarantees change. The forces defending the status quo remain powerful. Budget constraints limit new investment. NIMBY (Not In My Back Yard) opposition blocks treatment facilities. Civil liberties organizations continue to oppose expanded commitment authority. And the severely mentally ill themselves cannot vote, cannot organize, cannot advocate for their own interests. They depend entirely on others to speak for them. But the trajectory is not hopeless. The conditions for reform may be emerging, if slowly and unevenly.

WHAT REFORM WOULD REQUIRE

Building a system that actually works would require action on multiple fronts legal, financial, political, and cultural.

Legal reform must come first. The commitment standards established in the 1970s must be revised to allow intervention before a crisis becomes a catastrophe. The "imminent danger" standard must give way to criteria that permit treatment when someone is deteriorating, unable to care for themselves, or lacking the capacity for informed decisions about their care. This requires legislation at the state level, litigation to establish new precedents, and sustained advocacy to shift the legal culture.

Financial investment must follow. The infrastructure described in Chapter 10 adequate hospital capacity, residential facilities, ACT teams, supportive housing cannot be built without substantial new funding. Some of this can come from redirecting money currently wasted on ineffective crisis response. But much of it will require new appropriations, which means convincing legislators and taxpayers that the investment is worth making.

Political coalitions must be built. Reform will require bringing together groups that don't always agree: conservatives who want to restore public order, progressives who want to expand social services, families who want to save their loved ones, clinicians who want to treat their patients, law enforcement who want alternatives to arrest, and community members who want their neighborhoods back. Finding common ground among these constituencies is the work of political leadership.

Cultural attitudes must shift. The stigma that surrounds mental illness the belief that it's a moral failing, a weakness of character, something shameful to hide must be confronted and overcome. This is the work of education, of media representation, of public figures speaking openly about their own experiences or their families' experiences. Cultural change is slow, but it creates the conditions in which policy change becomes possible.

None of this will happen quickly. The system we have was built over decades; replacing it will take decades more. There will be setbacks, failed experiments, and unintended consequences. The history traced in this book should make us humble about our ability to design perfect solutions. What we can do is commit to building something better than what we have and to learning from our mistakes as we go.

A PERSONAL NOTE

I am seventy-nine years old, a retired clinical psychologist now living in Los Angeles. For more than fifty years, I have thought about these issues and I still cannot stop seeing diagnoses on the sidewalk. I will not live to see this crisis resolved.

I have written this book for those who will carry this work forward: the clinicians who treat the severely mentally ill, the families who love them, the advocates who fight for them, the policymakers who will shape the systems that serve them. I have tried to provide a framework historical, scientific, moral, and practical that might be useful in the decades ahead.

I have also written it as an act of witness. Someone who saw the old system at its worst, who watched it empty without alternatives, who has driven through the streets of Los Angeles for twenty-five years watching the consequences unfold someone should say what happened. Someone should name what we have done and what we have failed to do. Someone should insist that this is not acceptable, that human beings deserve better, that a wealthy and capable nation can do better if it chooses.

I think of the patients I evaluated in Ohio the catatonic woman, the man who hadn't spoken in years, the forgotten people in the locked wards. Many of them are long dead. But their successors are on the streets of every American city, exhibiting the same symptoms, suffering the same fate. The settings have changed; the illness has not.

I think of Rosemary Kennedy, lobotomized at 23, hidden for decades, her life sacrificed to her father's ambition and a system that enabled such destruction. Her brother tried to build something better. He failed, or rather, his vision was betrayed after his death. But the effort was worth making. The effort is always worth making.

I think of the families I have known, the parents who spent their savings trying to save their children, the siblings who gave up their own lives to caregiving, the spouses who endured years of chaos before the illness finally drove them away. They deserve a system that helps them rather than abandons them. They deserve to be partners in care rather than obstacles to autonomy.

THE ASYLUM WITHOUT WALLS

The title of this book is meant as an indictment. We have created an asylum without walls a system that provides none of the asylum's protections while imposing all of its exclusions. The severely mentally ill are still separated from society, still denied full participation in community life, still dying young. They're just doing it outdoors now, in plain view, while we avert our eyes and tell ourselves it's freedom.

But the title also points toward a goal. An asylum, in its original meaning, was a place of refuge a sanctuary where the vulnerable could find safety from a world that would harm them. The word comes from the Greek asylon, meaning "inviolable" or "safe from seizure." Before it became associated with locked wards and forced treatment, asylum meant protection.

What we need to build is a new kind of asylum, not a return to the old institutions, but a system that provides genuine refuge without walls. A system where the severely mentally ill can find safety, treatment, and dignity in the least restrictive setting appropriate to their condition. A system where responsibility is inescapable, and care is guaranteed. A system that recognizes both the reality of severe mental illness and the humanity of those who suffer from it.

Building such a system is the work of a generation. It will require changing laws, building infrastructure, shifting culture, and sustaining political will through the inevitable setbacks and disappointments. It will require money, effort, and persistence over decades.

But it is possible. Other nations have done it. Elements of it exist in scattered programs across America. The knowledge, the resources, and the moral clarity all exist. What has been lacking is the collective will to act—the decision, as a society, that the suffering on our streets is not acceptable and that we will do what is necessary to end it.

THE WOMAN ON SPRING STREET

I want to end where I began with the woman on Spring Street, arguing with invisible tormentors, lost in a world that we cannot enter and she cannot escape.

I see her every time I drive through downtown Los Angeles. She's not always the same person; sometimes it's a man, sometimes young, sometimes old, but the symptoms are the same. The voices, the gestures, the disconnection from everything around them. The clinical picture I learned to read fifty years ago, playing out on a sidewalk instead of in a locked ward.

I cannot help her. I am no longer a treatment provider. I have no authority to intervene, no program to connect her to, no magic words that will break through her psychosis. I can only watch, and remember, and bear witness.

But someone could help her. A system could be built that would reach her before she spent years on the street, before the accumulated brain damage made recovery impossible, before her body gave out from malnutrition and exposure and untreated infection. A system that would provide treatment even when she couldn't ask for it, housing even when she didn't know she needed it, care even when her illness told her to refuse.

That system doesn't exist today. But it could exist tomorrow if we decide to build it.

The woman on Spring Street is waiting. She doesn't know she's waiting; her illness has stolen that knowledge from her. But she's waiting nonetheless—for a society that will treat her as a human being deserving of care, not an autonomous agent deserving of neglect. She has been waiting for fifty years. How much longer will we make her wait?

The asylum without walls must end. We must build something better, something that provides true asylum, true refuge, for those whose minds have failed them. We have the knowledge. We have the resources. We have a moral obligation.

What we need now is the will.

EPILOGUE
THE CHOICE WE CANNOT ESCAPE

Fifty-four years ago, I walked through locked doors at Athens State Hospital and encountered human beings whose minds had betrayed them patients I was trained to evaluate but powerless to truly help. The system was already in motion, already emptying the wards in the name of liberation. I watched those early discharges with the optimism of my generation. We believed we were ending an era of cruelty.

We were beginning one.

The preceding chapters have documented what that optimism produced. We have traced the arc from Kirkbride's therapeutic vision through its corruption into warehousing. We have watched the community mental health movement promise everything and deliver almost nothing. We have followed the legal revolution that redefined abandonment as autonomy, the financial incentives that made discharge irresistible, and the cultural forces that made any form of institutional care politically radioactive. We have seen what other nations built while America dismantled. We have confronted what now fills our streets and jails—the living evidence of five decades of failure.

Now, at seventy-nine, I drive through Los Angeles and see the same symptoms I documented in Ohio played out on sidewalks. The catatonia, the command hallucinations, the slow destruction of minds we could treat but choose not to. The patients have not changed. Only their address has from the locked ward to the open pavement.

This is where the witness must become the verdict.

A NECESSARY CLARIFICATION

Before rendering that verdict, I must state clearly what this book's evidence shows: that the vast majority of people with mental illness are not violent. This is not a rhetorical gesture toward balance; it is a statistical fact. Most violence in society is committed by people without a diagnosable mental illness. People with depression, anxiety, bipolar disorder, and even schizophrenia are far more likely to be victims of violence than perpetrators, eleven times more likely, the research shows.

But we have also seen what happens when severe psychosis goes untreated for years. We have met the "known wolves" individuals with dozens of arrests, documented threats, trajectories of escalation visible to everyone except the legal system that could have intervened. The woman burned alive on the subway. The strangers pushed onto the tracks. The families watched helplessly as the illness progressed toward tragedy.

These outcomes are not inevitable. They are the predictable consequence of a system that treats intervention as the greater evil. Treatment protects everyone: the person who is ill, their family, and the public. The failure to treat protects no one.

WHAT THE EVIDENCE NOW DEMANDS

We began this book by asking how humanity has responded to the unchanging reality of severe mental illness. We found that every civilization that humanely managed this population did so by assigning clear responsibility for care, and every civilization that failed did so by allowing responsibility to be escaped.

The bimaristans of the Islamic golden age worked because someone was accountable for every patient. The Kirkbride asylums, before their corruption, worked because the state accepted responsibility for those who could not care for themselves. The Dutch FACT teams work today because regional authorities cannot discharge patients to nowhere. In every functioning system, past and present, responsibility is structurally embedded in law and institution, not dependent on individual charity or family endurance.

America alone has built a system where responsibility can always be escaped. The hospital discharges; its job is done. The shelter refuses; someone else's problem. The family exhausts itself and gives up; understandable. The state declines to fund; budgets are tight. At every point, an exit. And every exit leads to the same place: the street.

We have seen the neuroscience now—the PET scans showing reduced prefrontal activity during psychosis, the biological substrate of anosognosia visible on a screen. We can no longer pretend that a person refusing treatment is making an informed choice when the illness itself has damaged the brain regions required for insight. Science has settled what was once philosophical speculation. The question is whether our law and policy will acknowledge what our imaging technology has proven.

We have seen the medications that work—the long-acting injectables that maintain therapeutic levels for weeks, the pharmacogenomic testing that identifies optimal treatments, the clozapine that remains tragically underused because its monitoring requirements are impossible on the streets. The tools exist. They gather dust while people die.

We have seen what happens when intervention comes early versus late. The fifteen-fold reduction in homicide risk after treatment of first-episode psychosis. The progressive brain damage that accumulates with each untreated week of psychosis. We know that time matters, that delay is not neutral but destructive. We know this, and we delay anyway.

THE BINARY WE MUST FINALLY REJECT

Throughout this book, we have encountered the same false choice: the snake pits of the past or the sidewalks of the present. Nurse Ratched or Skid Row. Total confinement or total freedom.

Having traced its origins in legitimate reaction to institutional abuse, in civil libertarian ideology, in political convenience, in the cultural weight of One Flew Over the Cuckoo's Nest, we can finally name this binary for what it is: a refusal to build what lies between.

The Netherlands built what lies between. Germany built it. Italy, after abolishing its asylums completely, built replacement systems that actually function. Japan maintains the capacity we have abandoned. These nations did not solve mental illness. They simply refused to let the perfect become the enemy of the possible. They accepted that some people need protection they cannot request, care they will not initially welcome, and structure they lack the capacity to provide for themselves.

We have seen what freedom without capacity actually looks like. The woman eating from dumpsters is not exercising liberty; her illness is making choices her healthy self would never make. The man frozen in psychosis under the freeway did not weigh his options and select this life; his brain has been hijacked by disease. To call this autonomy is to empty the word of meaning. To call respecting it compassion is to make compassion complicit in cruelty.

THE FAMILIES WHO CANNOT FORGET

Behind the statistics and policy failures documented in these pages stand the families, the parents who spent retirement savings on treatments that failed, the siblings who organized their lives around crisis management, the children who grew up unable to bring friends home.

These families have been told they are "enabling" if they help, "abandoning" if they step back. They have been locked out by privacy laws, even when their loved one is too psychotic to recognize family members as family. They have called for help and been told that nothing can be done not until someone is hurt, not until the danger is "imminent," not until the preventable tragedy has already occurred.

247

The elderly parents haunt me most. I have heard their terrible prayer: that their child dies before they do. This is not cruelty. It is the devastating clarity of people who understand that when they are gone, there is no one left, and the street is waiting.

The current system has abandoned these families as surely as it has abandoned the ill themselves. Any system worthy of the name must include them—not as obstacles to patient autonomy but as partners in care, sources of history and context, people with standing to seek help for loved ones who cannot seek it themselves.

THE COST OF CONTINUATION

The alternative to building what this book proposes is not neutrality. The alternative is what we have now.

It is two thousand five hundred homeless deaths per year in Los Angeles County alone, average age of forty-six. It is thirty-two years of life erased per person not by disease alone but by our refusal to treat it.

It is emergency rooms boarding psychiatric patients for days because the beds do not exist. It is jails that have become the largest psychiatric facilities in the nation, not because they are suited to the task but because we have made them the only institution that cannot refuse admission.

It is the return of medieval diseases to American cities: typhus, hepatitis A, tuberculosis spreading through encampments that lack the sanitation infrastructure of a refugee camp.

It is children walking to school past human beings in florid psychosis, learning to step around bodies on sidewalks, developing the skill of not seeing that we have all been forced to acquire.

It is the billions we already spend on crisis response, on emergency care, on incarceration, on homeless services that manage without solving, scattered across systems that do not communicate, producing outcomes that benefit no one.

This is not the absence of policy. This is a policy of organized abandonment, maintained by inertia and political cowardice, protected by civil libertarian rhetoric that has been stretched far beyond its legitimate bounds.

THE CHOICE

We have arrived where this book always intended to bring us: to a choice we cannot evade by looking away.

The man I described in the Prologue lying in his own waste on Skid Row, screaming at tormentors only he can see will die on that street. This is not speculation; it is actuarial certainty. We have documented in these pages exactly why he will die there: the legal standards that prevent intervention, the beds that do not exist, the medications that cannot reach him, the system designed to ensure that responsibility can always be escaped.

His death will be recorded as "homeless mortality." No one will note that he could have been saved, that we possess the knowledge, the treatments, the resources to help him but chose not to because helping would require building systems we have decided not to build.

The blueprint exists. We have described it: the bed capacity at every level of care, the FACT teams and street psychiatry, the legal standards that replace "imminent danger" with frameworks that allow intervention before tragedy, the structural safeguards against the degradation that destroyed earlier systems. Other nations prove it can be built. Our own history includes moments when we built systems of care, however imperfect. The question is not whether this is possible. The question is whether we will choose to do it.

I am a clinician, not a politician or a prophet. I cannot tell you how to summon the political will that has been absent for sixty years. I cannot promise that what we build will not be corrupted by the same forces that corrupted what came before. I can only say that the knowledge exists, that the treatments exist, that the evidence of what works is documented in these pages and demonstrated in nations that chose differently than we have chosen.

A FINAL WITNESS

I am seventy-nine years old. I will not see this crisis resolved in my lifetime. The systems I have proposed, if built tomorrow, would take a decade to mature. The legal changes would face years of litigation. The cultural shift required from autonomy-as-abandonment to responsibility-as-care may take a generation.

But I can do what I have done in these pages: bear witness to what I have seen across fifty-four years, name what I have observed, describe what I believe must be built. This book is that witness. These chapters are that naming. The proposals are that description.

The severely mentally ill have always been with us. They will always be with us. The portion of humanity whose minds fracture beyond self-repair—roughly one to two percent

251

across all cultures and all recorded history—is not a problem we can solve. It is a reality we must accommodate. The only question is whether we will accommodate it with care or with abandonment dressed as freedom.

The pendulum that has swung between warehousing and neglect must finally find its center. Between the asylum that became a snake pit and the street that has become an open-air asylum lies the answer we have refused to seek: treatment. Structured care for those who need it. Supported independence for those who can achieve it. A continuum that does not require catastrophe as the price of admission.

I do not know who will champion this cause. I do not know what coalition of families and clinicians and reformed civil libertarians and brave politicians will finally say: enough. I only know that the evidence is here, in these pages, and that the people dying on our streets cannot wait for us to become comfortable with the solutions that might save them.

The asylum without walls must end.

What replaces it is our choice to make and after the evidence documented in this book, we can no longer pretend we do not know what that choice requires. The woman on

Spring Street, frozen in catatonia while the city flows around her, is waiting for that choice.

She has been waiting for fifty years.

REFERENCES

COURT CASES

Addington v. Texas, 441 U.S. 418 (1979).

Lessard v. Schmidt, 349 F. Supp. 1078 (E.D. Wis. 1972).

O'Connor v. Donaldson, 422 U.S. 563 (1975).

Rogers v. Okin, 478 F. Supp. 1342 (D. Mass. 1979).

Wyatt v. Stickney, 344 F. Supp. 387 (M.D. Ala. 1972).

LEGISLATION AND GOVERNMENT DOCUMENTS

Community Mental Health Centers Act of 1963, Pub. L. No. 88-164, 77 Stat. 282.

Lanterman-Petris-Short Act, Cal. Welf. & Inst. Code §§ 5000-5550 (1967).

Legge 180/1978 [Law 180] (Italy).

Omnibus Budget Reconciliation Act of 1981, Pub. L. No. 97-35, 95 Stat. 357.

Stewart B. McKinney Homeless Assistance Act of 1987, Pub. L. No. 100-77, 101 Stat. 482.

U.S. Government Accountability Office. (1977). Returning the mentally disabled to the community: Government needs to do more. GAO.

BOOKS AND MONOGRAPHS

Appelbaum, P. S. (1994). Almost a revolution: Mental health law and the limits of change. Oxford University Press.

Dix, D. L. (1843). Memorial to the Legislature of Massachusetts. Munroe & Francis.

Frank, R. G., & Glied, S. A. (2006). Better but not well: Mental health policy in the United States since 1950. Johns Hopkins University Press.

Goffman, E. (1961). Asylums: Essays on the social situation of mental patients and other inmates. Anchor Books.

Grob, G. N. (1994). The mad among us: A history of the care of America's mentally ill. Free Press.

Ibn Sina (Avicenna). (1025). Al-Qanun fi al-Tibb [The canon of medicine]. AMS Press.

Isaac, R. J., & Armat, V. C. (1990). Madness in the streets: How psychiatry and the law abandoned the mentally ill. Free Press.

Kesey, K. (1962). One flew over the cuckoo's nest. Viking Press.

Kirkbride, T. S. (1854). On the construction, organization, and general arrangements of hospitals for the insane. Lindsay & Blakiston.

Kramer, H., & Sprenger, J. (1487). Malleus maleficarum [The hammer of witches]. Dover Publications.

Lipset, S. M. (1996). American exceptionalism: A double-edged sword. W. W. Norton.

Porter, R. (2002). Madness: A brief history. Oxford University Press.

Shorter, E. (1997). A history of psychiatry: From the era of the asylum to the age of Prozac. John Wiley & Sons.

Szasz, T. S. (1961). The myth of mental illness: Foundations of a theory of personal conduct. Harper & Row.

Torrey, E. F. (1988). Nowhere to go: The tragic odyssey of the homeless mentally ill. Harper & Row.

Torrey, E. F. (2014). American psychosis: How the federal government destroyed the mental illness treatment system. Oxford University Press.

Turner, F. J. (1893). The significance of the frontier in American history. American Historical Association.

JOURNAL ARTICLES

De Girolamo, G., & Cozza, M. (2000). The Italian psychiatric reform. International Journal of Law and Psychiatry, 23(3-4), 197-214.

Elbogen, E. B., & Johnson, S. C. (2009). The intricate link between violence and mental disorder. Archives of General Psychiatry, 66(2), 152-161.

Fazel, S., et al. (2009). Schizophrenia and violence: Systematic review and meta-analysis. PLoS Medicine, 6(8), e1000120.

Lamb, H. R., & Bachrach, L. L. (2001). Some perspectives on deinstitutionalization. Psychiatric Services, 52(8), 1039-1045.

Mechanic, D., & Rochefort, D. A. (1990). Deinstitutionalization: An appraisal of reform. Annual Review of Sociology, 16(1), 301-327.

Steadman, H. J., et al. (2009). Prevalence of serious mental illness among jail inmates. Psychiatric Services, 60(6), 761-765.

Van Veldhuizen, J. R. (2007). FACT: A Dutch version of ACT. Community Mental Health Journal, 43(4), 421-433.

REPORTS AND POLICY DOCUMENTS

Los Angeles County Department of Public Health. (2023). Report on homeless mortality in Los Angeles County.

OECD. (2021). Health at a glance 2021: OECD indicators. OECD Publishing.

Treatment Advocacy Center. (2016). Going, going, gone: Trends and consequences of eliminating state psychiatric beds.

Treatment Advocacy Center. (2022). Grading the states: An analysis of U.S. psychiatric treatment laws.

World Health Organization. (2021). Mental health atlas 2020.

HISTORICAL SOURCES

Ebers Papyrus. (ca. 1550 BCE). Levin & Munksgaard.

Hippocrates. (ca. 400 BCE). On the sacred disease. Penguin Classics.

Kennedy, J. F. (1963, February 5). Special message to the Congress on mental illness and mental retardation.

Maisel, A. Q. (1946, May 6). Bedlam 1946. Life Magazine, 102-118.

MEDIA

Forman, M. (Director). (1975). One flew over the cuckoo's nest [Film]. United Artists.

Rivera, G. (Producer). (1972). Willowbrook: The last great disgrace [Television broadcast]. WABC-TV.

ABOUT THE AUTHOR

Dr. Ivan Gulas brings a unique perspective to America's mental health crisis, shaped by an extraordinary career trajectory from decades as a clinician in Boston to the executive suites of Hollywood studios, and now as a witness to the consequences of failed policy on the streets of Los Angeles.

He pursued graduate studies at Dartmouth College and earned his doctorate in Clinical Psychology from Ohio University. During his doctoral training in the 1970s, he worked directly with patients in large state psychiatric hospitals as the historic deinstitutionalization movement unfolded, observing firsthand the emptying of asylums that would fundamentally reshape mental health care in America.

He completed his clinical internship at Beth Israel Hospital, Harvard Medical School. As a Board-Certified Clinical Psychologist, he maintained a private clinical practice in Boston while serving on the faculty of Harvard Medical School for over two decades. He was also a staff psychologist at a private inpatient psychiatric hospital in Boston and provided neuropsychological evaluations at McLean Psychiatric Hospital, an affiliate of Massachusetts General

Brigham and one of the nation's premier psychiatric institutions.

Dr. Gulas co-founded Mirage Technologies in Boston with partners, including an MIT professor who pioneered telerobotic and minimally invasive surgical technologies. The company initially focused on developing innovative medical products but gained Hollywood's attention after creating breakthrough photorealistic CGI facial and tissue wrinkling capabilities—essential for realistic emotional expressions—for which Dr. Gulas was granted a U.S. patent.

With venture capital funding, they acquired a top Hollywood post-production facility, which, under Dr. Gulas's day-to-day leadership, greatly expanded in size and production capabilities. The company participated in major visual effects-driven projects, including Titanic and From the Earth to the Moon, earning an Emmy nomination. In a feature article, WIRED magazine recognized Dr. Gulas as one of 25 players reinventing entertainment.

In 2000, he permanently relocated to Los Angeles, where he has been producing live events, television series, and feature films. He is a member of the Producers Guild of America. While he transitioned his career from direct clinical services, he continued to consult and publish on clinical issues.

He is the author of *Changing The Odds: A New Understanding of PTSD and a Path to Recovery*, published in 2025.

Now seventy-nine years old, Dr. Gulas finds that every drive through Venice, Hollywood, or downtown Los Angeles becomes a diagnostic exercise he cannot turn off. The psychiatric symptoms he learned to recognize in those Ohio wards fifty years ago are now visible on sidewalks rather than in locked facilities. This book represents his effort to bear witness to what he has observed across five decades—and to articulate what must be built to replace the asylum without walls that America has created.

www.ingramcontent.com/pod-product-compliance
Lightning Source LLC
Chambersburg PA
CBHW030409130626
46549CB00004B/1688